No Shame in Fear

Alex C. Maclean

Islands Book Trust

Published in 2016 by the Islands Book Trust

www.theislandsbooktrust.com

ISBN: 978-1-907443-71-8

Islands Book Trust
Laxay Hall
Laxay
Isle of Lewis
HS2 9PJ
Tel: 01851 830316

Typeset by Erica Schwarz (www.schwarz-editorial.co.uk)
Cover design by Raspberry Creative Type, Edinburgh
Printed and bound by Martins the Printers, Berwick upon Tweed

Contents

Introduction

There are a number of reasons why readers gain pleasure from books. For some, the appeal is based simply on the content of the work. There is the swirl of adventure, the tremor of love and romance, the puzzle of attempting to decide 'who' or 'why' someone 'dun it', solving the puzzle the writer has generated through some particular crime, the St Valentine's Day massacre that took place, say, in the shops of Scarinish or Stornoway. There are, too, the works that give the reader the essence of a time or place, whether that be the Second World War or the Spanish Inquisition. In these kind of books, the sense of atmosphere is all. It is often created by the gathering together of small details, enough to convince the reader that they are witnessing someone who is the middle of the Battle of Stalingrad or suffering torture in a prison cell in Seville at the end of the fifteenth century.

Alex Maclean's work is nothing like that. It works in a very different way from any of these models, gaining its power from its sincerity, the conviction we hear from the consistency of his own personal voice. In this, it has much in common with speech. It is the same conversational tone to which we listen when he relates to us the facts and realities of his own childhood, being brought up by his mother in Cornaigmore in Tiree, as the voice we encounter again when he describes the realities of ageing, how life is narrowing and closing around him compared to the open horizons of his younger days. The contrast is there – as anyone will testify who knows the exposed nature of the shoreline of that inner Hebridean isle, one to which many of my forebears belong, but the rhythm and the language stay very much the same. Strike it, like the Ringing Stone that stands in Bailephetrish in Tiree, and its tone and pitch are strong and true.

It is also in some ways, however, not just the tale of an individual, but the story of many of those who were his contemporaries both in Tiree and elsewhere in the Highlands and Islands. There was the shame of his own illegitimacy, that secret so many of his counterparts scattered throughout the Hebrides and beyond nurtured in their souls. It had a crippling and belittling effect with mothers, grandparents and others unable to pass onto their offspring the truth behind their arrival on this earth. The silence and pretence this engendered had a stifling, negative effect on all their relationships, sometimes into adult life. For all that a few might argue otherwise, it is one of the positive effects of the sexual revolution on our generation that such arrivals are no longer greeted with the hush and horror they were at one time. There are fewer judgements whispered behind fingers, far less grunts and tuts of disapproval when a woman with a child born out of wedlock enters the village shop.

And then there are the other aspects of Alex's life that ripple out, touching others. His tale of being on the SS *Siris* when it was torpedoed and sunk in July 1942 mirrors one of the few stories I heard from the lips of my own Skye grandfather, another Alex. (He told with particular relish the story of a Glaswegian 'hard man' who was on the lifeboat with them. 'He was crying for his Mammy five minutes after the ship went down'.) Again, there are no swaggering heroics, just simple understatement about the predicament they were in. One can only wish that all our heroes were as quiet and reticent as that.

Another aspect of Alex Maclean's life that impressed me was his commitment to democratic Socialism, one that later edged into his Christian faith and belief. It was a pattern that was familiar to me in my own youth, from watching my Dad and others, who were engaged in the politics of Trade Unions in their early existence, before becoming involved in the Church later. It seems to me that many of these activities – particularly in the north of Scotland but also in places like Methodist Wales – stem from similar roots, similar in the way in which the idea of service to others, humility and solidarity with the community are emphasised and valued. No doubt both men would look on with sadness at how that tradition has dwindled and faltered in recent years, not just in Scotland and Britain but across Western Europe as a whole. (One could in fact argue that it has even affected the number of splits and secessions found within the Presbyterian churches. Individuality is all; community and compromise are devalued and sold short.) It is tempting, too, to conclude that in Alex's case, it was motivated by a sharp sense of the injustice he suffered as a young child, without a father to guide, help and protect him in a community where other people's lives seemed uniform and stable.

It might have been this, too, that motivated Alex when at the early age of 37, his wife passed away. Like my own father, he brought up his children, Jean, Ronald and Alexandra, alone from this point onwards, guarding and protecting them while being aware – like my Dad was from time to time – of his inadequacies at being forced to play the roles of both parents. Once again, he would have been conscious of the judgements whispered behind hands, the tuts of disapproval that might have accompanied his efforts, that sense he may have possessed that no matter how good a parent he might strive to be, as a man he simply wasn't 'good enough'. Only three individuals in the world can afford, however, to judge Alex on the worth and value of his example while undertaking this task – and one of them, Jean, passed away a number of years ago. I feel sure that the remaining two will cast their judgement and look upon him with great love and respect.

For there is little doubt, when reading this book, that Alex Maclean, though blessed with great love, had a tough and difficult life, one that came to end at the age of 66, six years after his existence became closed in by the lengthening walls and shadows of Alzheimer's.

There is little doubt either that he did his level best to break through.

DONALD S. MURRAY

September 2016

Chapter One

Tiree Boyhood

My earliest recollections as a small child are of lying in my bed in the pitch darkness listening to the howling of the wind around our small tin house and of hailstones battering against galvanised sheeting until I thought the end of the world must come. Or maybe, on a calm night, I would listen to the thunder of the waves as they crashed on the silver sands of the nearby shore.

Very often, when the wind got really bad in the winter months, my mother and I would leave the house and spend the night in the nearby byre. Although we felt safer from the storm because of the thick stone walls, it was anything but comfortable, being draughty and dark. The occasional stamping of the cattle accompanied by the scurrying and squealing of rats made me wish that my mother would remain in the house, storm or no storm. However she was convinced that the frail tin house would, some night, be picked up by that shrieking wind and hurled into the sea. Who could have blamed her, for on this small, flat island of Tiree, lying out in the Atlantic off the west coast of Scotland, gusts of upwards of eighty miles an hour were commonplace in winter. Our house was situated over a mile from the nearest occupied house and so, on those dark and stormy winter nights, it was an eerie place indeed.

My mother and I lived alone, for I was an only child. It seemed my father had died when I was a baby. My mother was a small, frail woman, and deeply religious. She kept us both by knitting jumpers, socks, shawls; you name it, she would knit it and sell it. She never failed to take first prize in any knitting contest she entered, but she had only one pair of hands and her health was indifferent. There were many days she could not knit, and so we starved. Often she would do without food so that I could eat, and by doing so she would also have enough money left to buy paraffin for the lamp, which would enable her to sit up all night to complete an order. She would call me at five in the morning when she had the parcel ready for posting. With the parcel in a haversack across my shoulders I would step out into the darkness and battle my way against the howling wind along two miles of lonely road to where I would meet the postman with his lorry. He would see that the precious parcel caught the mail boat, which sailed south to Oban.

From as far back as I can remember I could do any of the household chores. I had to, as my mother must knit. When I came home from school my first job was to see to the lamp. I would check it had oil, clean the glass funnel and trim the wick. Then I would search the shore for coke and driftwood, which were plentiful, so though we had little else we always had a good fire.

Our little house, though poor, was spotless. It had bare wooden floors which were scrubbed pure white with sand from the beach. There was a stove about four feet long which was my pride and joy. I would black lead it and polish it and emery the steels till they shone like mirrors. There was a water pump about fifty yards from the house, and all the water had to be carried in. It was at this pump that I washed myself summer and winter, often surrounded by cattle. Little did I know, in those early days, how all this training would be of such good use to me in later years.

When I was about nine years old I began to work on the surrounding farms after school, at weekends and in the school holidays. My payment was in kind: if I was lifting potatoes I would be given as many potatoes as I could carry home at the end of each day; if I helped to churn the butter I would bring home a huge lump; and if I helped with the milking I would bring home milk, and so on. It was in this way that I got my first bicycle. I worked for a full month cleaning out the byre, feeding the horses and doing all the tasks connected with the running of a farm, and at the end of the month the old farmer asked me to accompany him into the barn, where there lay an old rusty bicycle half covered in hay. It had no brakes or mudguards.

"Laddie," said the old farmer, "you have worked hard and well, so as a little extra that cycle is yours. Take it away home with you."

I will never forget the joy and pride I felt as I cycled home that night. I know that even today if I could buy the most expensive car in the world it could never take the place of that old lump of junk.

My mother was devoted to me, and I in turn loved and admired her, so although life was hard I was very happy. I loved my beautiful island with its magnificent beaches and clear blue sea lapping the silver sands. In winter I watched the giant waves with their white tops come riding in to crash into a million pieces of silver spray. There was something awe-inspiring that seemed to draw me like a magnet to the beach on a stormy day. I had a special rock on which I would sit for hours, just watching that angry sea.

On a dark frosty night I loved to look up at the velvety sky where millions of stars stood out like fabulous jewels, and shooting stars flew about the sky like fireworks. On these winter nights I used to visit the surrounding crofts and join in the *ceilidhs*, this being the Gaelic word for concert. We would all gather round a huge fire where someone would have a fiddle or some other instrument and each one of us in turn would sing a Gaelic song. After the singing was over someone would start to tell ghost stories, mostly about the island itself. This was alright while we were all together, but many a night when I had to go home alone over the pitch dark fields I would look over my shoulder to see if there were any ghosts following me.

While the ceilidh was in progress the lady of the house would be busy baking scones, pancakes and potato scones. The aroma was indeed inviting, and so to finish off the evening we would be served with tea and hot buttered scones. They were delicious.

And so the short winter days with their long, dark, stormy nights would give way to spring. The air filled with the smell of the newly ploughed fields. The snow white lambs bounded and skipped after their mothers. I loved wandering over the green fields, where the daisies and buttercups made a riot of colour. I would stop at one of the many small streams and drink from its crystal clear cold water until I thought my lungs would burst. Looking up, I could see dotted all over the island the small crofts with their thatched cottages whose whitewashed walls glistered in the sun.

In turn spring gave way to the long, hot summer days, with the fields in all their different shades of gold, brown and green, and the barley, oats and corn swaying in the breeze. The bees hummed as they went about their task, and I admired the multitude of colours of the hundreds of butterflies as they flitted from flower to flower.

Then would come the autumn and the fields now shorn of their crops were dotted with ricks of hay waiting to be taken back to the farmyard where they would be built into the huge haystacks which would feed the cattle during the winter months. The smell of the new mown hay was always something that reminded one it was indeed autumn and that it was time to search the shores for driftwood to be dried and stored for those oncoming winter nights.

One of my great loves was animals, and I became pretty expert at handling them. On one occasion a cat died, leaving three day-old kittens. The crofter I was working with at the time was going to drown them but I pleaded with him to let me take them home. I got a goose feather and cut the stalk off. I then snipped off one end and this left me with a hollow tube. Filling my mouth with milk I put one end of the tube into my mouth and the other end into the tiny mouth of each kitten in turn. Then I controlled the feed of milk down the tube into the kittens' mouths. They survived to grow into three beautiful cats.

In the lambing season I would roam the fields looking for sheep which were having trouble giving birth. I would kneel down beside the sheep and speaking to it as a doctor would to a patient, I would roll up my sleeve and assist the lamb into the world. Many a scolding I got from my mother when I arrived home covered in blood, very often with a newly born lamb in my arms. I would plead with her to allow me to keep it at the fire overnight and she never refused. So, wrapped in a sack, it would lie by the fire, and in the morning I would return it to its mother.

The school I attended was very old and its grey stone walls had a weather-beaten appearance from all the years of buffeting by the northern gales as they swept in from the nearby Atlantic. Inside it was cosy, each classroom having a large fireplace. Around the fire was a huge fireguard, and in winter it was usual to see this draped with steaming clothes. Some of the pupils had to walk as far as six miles across the moors to get to school, sometimes in howling gales and lashing rain, hence the clothes on the fireguard. In those days we carried our sandwiches and tins of cocoa mixed with sugar and at the lunch break we would boil a kettle and eat our sandwiches with steaming cocoa. Though the school may sound rather primitive to the reader of today, there was nothing primitive about the education we received. There were as many doctors, ships' captains, ministers and vets turned out of that school as there are out of the most modern senior secondary school today.

As a child however I never liked school. I felt that it was all such a waste of time. While the teacher lectured us on this or that subject I gazed out of the window across the beautiful fields and wished I was out there working, or at other times just I sat and day-dreamed. My thoughts would drift off to the day when I would be a great sea captain, sailing my great ship all over the world, and bringing home all the beautiful things I could buy to my mother. I would buy her a beautiful big white house and she would have servants to look after her. Suddenly a voice would break into my thoughts and standing over me would be a very impatient teacher. He or she would ask me a question on the subject being discussed. Of course, I did not have a clue about the subject, never mind the answer, and so I would be taken out to the front of the class and given a few of the strap and then banished behind the blackboard in disgrace. I think I spent more of my time at school behind the blackboard than I did in front of it.

My constant day-dreaming and lack of interest in school did not endear me to my teachers. The strap became an everyday occurrence. Many times my fingers stung so badly that I wanted to cry, but there was another side to my nature – a stubbornness that would not let me give in. How could I tell those teachers that all I wanted to do was to work on those crofts and bring home butter, potatoes and meat? How could they in turn tell me that I could never be a sea captain without education, when they did not know of what I day-dreamed? Many times in my life I was to think of those teachers with great admiration and respect for what they had tried so hard to do for me. Yet I do not believe they failed, for they taught me many things that helped me in life.

As I grew older I became more restless. I was drawn more and more down to the sea. I would spend hours sitting on my favourite rock gazing across that sparkling sea at the other islands in the distance. They reminded me of other planets. I would look over at the Cuillin hills of Skye, which were always shrouded in mist at the top. They always reminded me of a giant's castle that reached all the way to heaven.

As I sat there I would take my mood from the sea. If it was angry and restless so my mood would be. I would wonder why we were so poor and why my mother had to work so hard? Why could I not have had a father like other children? Or brothers or sisters? What had my father been like and why did people never speak of him? Why was I so stubborn and restless? And then one particular day, a fortnight before my fourteenth birthday, the answer came to me as I sat on that rock. I wanted to see what lay beyond those islands in the distance and measure how far it was to the line where the sky met the sea. My mind was made up. I was going to sail that restless heaving sea until I found the answer.

As I sat that night and told my mother of my plans, the tears ran down her face. She tried to reason with me. She pointed out that I was only fourteen, with no knowledge of big cities and their dangers to one as young as I. Would I not stay at school for another year? But in the end she realised this was what I wanted and that my mind was made up. I wrote to a shipping company in Glasgow and a few days later I received a letter from them, inviting me to join one of their ships as a cabin boy. I was to join the ship in Glasgow in a week's time.

The day before I was due to leave the island I went down to the beach. This time my mother suggested that as it was my last day, she might come with me to see this rock of which I seemed to be so fond. So armed with a flask of tea and some scones, the two of us set off. When we arrived at the beach I guided my mother to the rock. On one side of it was a path made by the sheep as they climbed to the top, which was flat and covered in grass. The top measured about fifty yards by twenty yards. One could walk across to the seaward side and look down on the Atlantic crashing on the base of the rock about twenty feet below. When I came alone I sat at the edge with my legs dangling over the side, the spray hitting my face. On this occasion, however, we sat on the grass in the centre, with two or three sheep grazing around us. It was a beautiful April day, with the sun reflecting on the sea.

As we sat there together, having tea from the flask, my mother lectured me on the things I was to do and the things I was not to do. The advice she gave me that day was to carry me through some trying times in my life.

"Son," she said, "there is no shame in fear. We are all born with fear in us. The shame of your fear is in giving way to it. Some day you will be a man. People will look to you for comfort, perhaps when they are afraid, or perhaps when they are sick, or when they have lost someone very dear to them. Give them that comfort. Never let those people down. Grow up to be a man in whose hands people know they can put their lives with complete trust. And remember your word must always be accepted by your friends and your enemies alike. You may never become a sea captain, but remember and practise what I have said to you today and you will be a captain, a captain among men, and captain of your destiny. That, my son, is all that anyone can ask of life."

As we prepared to leave for home my mother looked at me strangely.

"There is something I must tell you son," she said. "It is something about you. I must, oh, I must." I saw how distressed she had become.

"Please wait. I want to have a last look at those islands before we go home, Mother," I said. I walked to the edge of the rock and gazed over to the Cuillin hills of Skye. The tops were misted, or was it the tears rolling down my cheeks, for I knew then that my mother had been about to tell me something. Was it about my father? Well, all that mattered in the world to me was that she was my mother. I looked at that line where the sky met the sea. Tomorrow I would sail those seas, and I would sail and sail till I reached that line. Returning to where my mother stood watching me, I put my arm around her.

"Come, mother, let us go home, and whatever it was you were going to tell me, please don't. Perhaps some other time."

The following morning I picked up my old, battered case with its meagre contents, had a last look round the little house and accompanied by my mother, stepped out into the cold dark morning. We made our way down the deserted road to meet the postman on his way to catch the mail boat. It was just like all the other mornings that I had done this since I was six years old, but this time I would not be going back to my little tin home. I began to feel rather frightened. This was the road I had walked so many hundreds of times to school, my schoolbooks slung over my shoulder with a leather strap. I thought of those winter mornings when I had bent almost double to battle against the wind, those spring and summer mornings I had marched down that road singing at the top of my voice; so poor, so happy, so alive. Those golden years of childhood had now gone forever. I was fourteen, and no longer a child.

By six-thirty my mother and I were waiting on the deserted, windswept pier. It would be touch and go whether the mail boat would attempt to make the pier that morning, because of the strong wind and rough sea. This was not unusual. Often our small island was marooned for days on end, when it was too stormy for the mail boat to enter the bay. As we looked out on that turbulent sea however, we could see the ship's mast lights. She was going to make it.

The boat came alongside, tied up and I realised with a terrible feeling of fear that the time had come to say goodbye. I didn't want to go. I wanted to return to my little home and never leave my beautiful island. What was it my mother had said? Something about there being no shame in fear, only in giving in to it. I turned and kissed my mother goodbye, then ran up the heaving gangway, choking back the tears I knew I must shed.

We cast away from the pier and swung round into the heavy seas. I stood at the stern, waving to the lonely, frail figure until the sea and the spray blotted her from sight. The tears rolled down my cheeks, burning my face like molten metal. I had a terrible feeling in my stomach. It was seasickness. How was I ever going to be a sailor?

Chapter Two

Cabin Boy

Stepping out of Buchanan Street Station I was frightened and bewildered. What kind of new world was this in which I found myself? Hundreds of people rushed this way and that; more than I had ever seen in my life before. Where were they all going and where had they all come from? What were those great sparkling, clanging monsters running along rails, full of people staring out of the windows? (I would later discover they were called tram cars.) There was a terrible roar of traffic and huge grey, grim buildings surrounded me. Where were the green fields? Where was the sea? How could I join a ship if there was no sea? Oh, I did not like this strange new world at all.

My mother had told me to get hold of the first policeman I saw. We had a policeman back home on the island, so I knew the uniform. I saw a huge man standing nearby wearing the same uniform, but he had a funny big helmet, not like the one the policeman wore back home. However, plucking up what little courage I had left, I approached the huge man.

"Excuse me, Sir. Are you a policeman?" I asked, looking up at that face towering above me.

"Are you trying to be cheeky, son?" came the reply.

"No, sir. My mother told me to ask a policeman the way to a place called the Broomielaw," I said.

"Oh, she did, did she? And may I ask where your mother is now?"

"She is back home. She couldn't afford the fare to come with me."

"And where is it you stay?" he asked.

"I stay in Tiree, sir."

"And where is that?"

"Well, sir, it's a small island off the west coast of Scotland. It must be near the island of Skye, for on a clear day you can see the Cuillin Hills," I replied.

"Well, well, you don't say, son. And what do you want to go to the Broomielaw for?"

"I am joining a ship, sir."

"You're what! You're joining a ship – as captain, no doubt!"

"No, sir, as cabin boy."

The policeman looked decidedly puzzled. Suddenly I remembered the letter in my pocket from the shipping company, telling me to join their ship. I took it out and showed it to the policeman.

"Well, well," said the policeman, "and I didn't believe a word of what you told me. I was sure you were running away. Have you had anything to eat?"

"No, sir. My mother gave me scones and four shillings. It was all she could afford and I didn't want to spend it."

"Well, son, just you come along with me."

He took me into a police station, and there he related my story to the Inspector, who took a great interest in me, asking me many questions about my boyhood. While this was going on, someone had gone out and bought me a fish supper and cakes, which I ate in what must have been the Inspector's office. After I had finished, the Inspector told me that there was a police car ready to take me down to my ship. As I took leave of all my newly made friends, the Inspector put ten shillings into my hand.

"Do you know, son," he said, "we get some bad smells about this place sometimes. In my job, my faith in mankind gets awfully strained. This office today smells beautiful. I can almost smell the sea and the country. Don't allow yourself to be changed by the evil and corruption of the big cities."

I clutched my ten shillings, which to me was a fortune. It seemed that they had had a whip round in the station. I entered the police car and was driven in style down to where my ship lay. With their kindness that day, the police made one of their most ardent fans. I have always had the greatest respect and admiration for them.

As the police car drove away I felt very alone and apprehensive. I walked through the big shed and onto the quayside, and there lay my new home. She was the biggest ship I had ever seen, but in actual fact she was only a medium sized general cargo coaster of about a thousand tons. Everything around me was hustle and bustle. Dockers were shouting and scurrying about all over the place. Winches were clattering and blowing out great columns of steam, and mighty cranes on the quayside were lifting great loads high in the air, swinging them over towards the ship and lowering them into a huge hole in the deck. I was fascinated yet frightened by all this terrible noise. Little did I know that day how much, in the years ahead, I would come to love the noise and intense activity of a ship in port.

I climbed the steep gangway and stepped on to the deck, where I saw a chap standing, watching the cargo being loaded. He had a gold band round his sleeve and brass buttons. Maybe he is the Captain, I thought, but I found out later he was the Second Officer. I approached him with great respect.

"Excuse me, sir. I was told to report to the cook-steward. Do you know where I will find him?" I asked.

"And what do you want to see that old bastard for?" he replied.

"Well, sir, I am the new galley boy," I said.

"Oh, God, no! Not another bloody one to poison us! Come on, I will take you to him."

"Hey, Drip," shouted the officer, sticking his head through the galley doorway, "here is another bloody galley boy for you. No wonder I have damned indigestion. You must be putting them in the stew! No wonder it tastes so bloody awful."

A thin old man with a shock of pure white hair and a dirty looking white jacket appeared at the door. Taking one look at me he let go a string of oaths, the like of which I had never heard before.

"I bloody ask you – what am I supposed to do with that? They are sending them now with their nappies still on. I am an old man. I need a big strong boy. Look at the size of him!" It was true I was small for my age, and looked younger than my fourteen years. The officer grinned all over his face.

"Well, Drip, you have one consolation. You will not have to cut him up to put him in the pot," he said.

"Just you get to hell and don't interfere with my catering staff. The only thing that has saved you from the pot is the fact that I cook only fresh meat. All officers are bloody rotten," came the reply. Still with a huge grin on his face, the officer turned about and went back the way we had come. I stood there not knowing what to do. The old man looked me up and down and shook his head.

"Well, boy, how long are you going to stand there gaping like a bloody fish on a fishmonger's slab. There is a lot of work to be done. Come and I will show you to your cabin."

We walked along the deck and stopped at a door. Above it were the words 'Cabin Boy'. He opened the door and there, facing me, was a beautiful bunk with snow white linen sheets. Below the bunk were six built in drawers, with brass handles on each drawer. The mahogany wood shone and reflected the gleaming brass handles. It was a small, compact cabin. Between the end of the bunk and the wash hand basin was a two-seater settee. I was to sail on many ships, in some of which the Captain did not have as nice a cabin as that which I had on my first little coaster.

"I will expect you along at the galley in ten minutes," said the cook. "Put your stuff away in those drawers. I expect you to keep this cabin as you found it. You will change the linen once a week. You will polish the brasses once a week. You will also use linseed oil when polishing the woodwork. I want you to listen while I tell you what your daily duties will consist of.

"You will be called at six every morning and the first thing you will do is make up your bunk. You will then go to the galley where you will make one slice of toast and one pint mug of tea which you will take up to the officer on the bridge not one minute later than six-thirty. If you are late then the officer will complain to the Captain who in turn will complain to me, and I in turn will kick you on the backside, and, depending on how I feel, I may even sack you. At seven you will call me. You will then set the officers' table for breakfast. When breakfast is ready you will serve the table. You will go to the Captain's cabin before eight in the morning with a mug of hot water for him to shave, and while he is shaving you will bring down his shoes and polish them. After breakfast you will make the Captain's bunk and dust out his cabin. You will wash up the dirty dishes, and so on. In the afternoon you will get an hour off. Your last duty at night will be at eight, when the officers get their supper. Now, for these small services you will be paid eight shillings a week, and all the food you can eat. I will show you all the things you need to know. Now, be in the galley in ten minutes."

"Yes, Sir," I replied.

"Don't call me 'Sir' again," came the reply, "on this ship I am known as 'the Drip'. Reserve the 'Sir' for those bloody officers. You know I have two pet hates in my life. One is officers and the other is damned galley boys." With that he turned and walked out, leaving me feeling very bewildered and rather frightened.

Those first months were like a nightmare to me. As we pitched and rolled through the Irish Sea and round the Bishop Rock I was terribly seasick. Sometimes I would crawl into some corner, feeling I must surely be dying. But the Drip would always find me. He would pull me out and, with a cuff on the ear, make me get on with the job.

"Get on with peeling those potatoes," he would say, "and if you want to be sick just be sick among the potatoes. They are for the officers anyway." I never found out why he disliked them so much. Sometimes one of the officers would complement him, perhaps on the soup.

"They won't enjoy it tomorrow," he would say to me with a wink. With that he would dump a big handful of salt into the pot.

Under the Drip's tuition I learned all the things that go towards making a first class ship's steward. He even taught me the finer arts of cooking. He knew every aspect of his job inside out. Gradually, as the months went by, I got over my seasickness, though I had still to get my sea legs. I staggered all over the place with the lurching of the ship.

One day, while serving the soup, I approached the Captain and just as I was about to lay his soup in front of him, the ship took a sudden roll. I lost my balance and instead of the soup landing on the table, it landed smack in the Captain's lap. On returning to the pantry, where I expected to be given a terrible telling off, I found the Drip in fits of laughter.

"Do you know son, you have just done something that I have dreamed about all my life? I always wanted to drop a plate of soup over an officer, but I never had the opportunity. But you got the jackpot, the Captain himself. Wonderful, bloody wonderful."

The crew were all from Glasgow and they were a real tough lot. There was big Harry, Charlie, Malkie and Joe, to mention but a few. They came from all over, from Anderson to the Gorbals. The officers did not like my mixing with them, but those rough, tough men looked after me as if I were one of their own sons. Instead of leading me astray, as the officers feared, they taught me how to look after myself, and how to keep out of trouble, though they themselves were never out of it. They always made sure that I had money to go to the pictures. I became known to those men as 'the laddie from the croft'.

On coastal vessels the officers, the cook and myself were fed by the shipping company. The sailors and stokers had to buy their own food and cook it on board. Usually they drank their money and so had few rations with them for the trip. Joe was one of my favourites. He was a stoker, or fireman, as they were known. He came from Anderson, one of the so-called tough areas of Glasgow. One day I decided I would smuggle a tin of fruit out of the pantry to give to him. That night, with the tin of fruit tucked under my jacket, I made my way down to the crew's quarters, where I handed it to Joe. To my amazement he was very angry.

"Just you take that back, and don't ever do a thing like that again," he said.

I was later to find out that Joe, like so many of the others, had been in prison on a few occasions for shoplifting and other offences. That was the type of men they were. Rough, tough and drunken members of society. Little was society to know how much they would owe to men like Joe in the years that lay ahead.

I bad been on the ship about three months when the Drip told me he had put me through for a rise, which would bring my wages up to twelve shillings a week. By this time I had found out why he was called the Drip. He smoked an old clay pipe which was seldom out of his mouth. The saliva would run down the stem, balance on the bottom of the bowl, then drip off, sometimes into the porridge.

I wrote to my mother once a week and sent her most of my wages. Sometimes, as I lay in my bunk in the darkness, listening to the crash of the angry sea on the bow and the whistle of the wind as it tore at the rigging, I would think of my little tin house which seemed to be so very far away. I would think of my mother and picture her sitting in the darkness of the byre alone, and I would feel terribly homesick.

When we docked in Glasgow after our ten day trip everyone would go home, leaving me alone on the ship, apart from an old watchman. As the dynamo was shut down in port at night all I had was an oil lamp. I used to lie on my bunk in the deserted ship, listening to the creak of the mooring ropes and the gentle lap of the water round the ship. Now and again I heard the squeal of rats running about the deck outside. It was very eerie and frightening.

Usually we spent two and sometimes three days in Glasgow, first unloading and then reloading for our next trip. As the officers did not dine on board in Glasgow and the Drip would be away for most of the time, he would leave me with all the keys so I had all the food I needed. One night a policeman came on board and asked me if I could lend him an old pot. He came from the Isle of Skye and wanted the pot to boil salt herring. He lived only five minutes' walk from the ship so each time the ship came in I lent him a pot. One day I was going through the dock shed with a cigarette somebody had given me. Though I didn't really smoke, I had lit up to make an impression. I saw a policeman approaching but I did not recognise him at first. When he reached me I saw it was my friend, looking very stern.

"Don't you know you are not allowed to smoke in these sheds?" he said. "I could send you to prison."

"Please, Sir," I replied, "if you do that where will you get a pot to boil your herrings?"

"Now, there is a point," replied the now grinning officer. "Don't smoke in here son. It is not allowed."

As time went on, the relationship between the Drip and myself changed. We were no longer the boss and the boy. I began to realise that he was quite fond of me, though outwardly he was still a gruff old man. One day I went into my cabin and there, lying on my bunk, was a brand new air gun. The Drip had bought it for me, but he would never admit to such weakness.

I had been on the ship about ten months and we were heading home to Glasgow, when the Drip told me of his intention to retire when we arrived, as he was now seventy years of age. He took me to his cabin and, pointing to his radio, told me it was now mine. He then told me that he had been so hard on me during those first voyages because it was the only way to get me over both my seasickness and my homesickness. As he put it, he had liked me from that first day he had stuck his head out of the galley door.

"Do you know, son, I went to sea when I was fourteen as a galley boy. I too was small for my age. You reminded me so much of that day over fifty years ago," he said.

The end of the trip arrived and we tied up in Glasgow. The Drip asked me to carry his suitcase off the ship. We shook hands in farewell in the dockside shed. As I took my hand away I discovered three pounds folded in it.

"I am the boss," he said, when I tried to reason with him. "Would you like a cuff on the ear?" He then turned and walked away. I stood and watched the old, stooped figure as it faded into the distance and once again I had that terrible feeling of being alone. That day, when I drew my wages, I had another surprise. The Drip had got me another rise, which brought my wages up to eighteen shillings a week, making me the youngest but highest paid galley boy in the Company's fleet of five ships.

I was delighted to receive a letter from my mother, asking me when I would be back in Glasgow, as she had saved enough money to come to see me. When we tied up in Glasgow after the next voyage, there she was, standing on the quay. It was a year since I had last seen her and it seemed such a long, long time. I think everybody on that ship knew who she was. As the crew went ashore every man in turn stopped to speak to her, even the Captain. I was so very proud that day. We spent three days together in Glasgow and I took her to cafes and cinemas. I wanted to show her that I was now a man of the big city. Too soon the time came for us to part again, my mother returning to her lonely, windswept island and I to my angry, windswept sea.

After spending eighteen months on this, my first ship, I decided I now had enough experience to spread my wings a bit, so I applied to a well-known shipping line which serviced the Western Isles. I joined one of their passenger mail boats as steward. I was not quite sixteen, still young to hold this position. My wages were now thirty shillings a week, so with my food supplied and tips from the passengers, I was doing very well. I began to make plans to bring my mother to stay in Glasgow for good.

I wrote, telling her of my idea and after a bit of correspondence, eventually got her to agree to my plans. After much searching I at last found an unfurnished room in the heart of the Gorbals. It was a small, drab room in a crumbling old tenement, but at least it would be a home where we could be together again between my trips. My mother had sent me a few pounds to buy some furniture and instructions on what to buy, so I scoured the second hand shops until I had all the necessities.

At last all was ready and I wrote home, giving her the address. I remember clearly my excitement as I climbed those crumbling tenement stairs. I wondered if she would like the room, but I need not have worried, for she was delighted. Thereafter, on my frequent visits to Glasgow I, like everyone else, had a home to come back to.

I had now given up the catering department and was sailing out of Glasgow as an ordinary seaman with another well-known firm of colliers. On these small ships I sailed all round the coast from John O' Groats to

Land's End. Life on board those colliers was really tough. Coal dust was everywhere, so I was always black. As on all coasters, I had to buy my own food, and cook and eat it when time permitted. At sea our watches were four hours on and four hours off duty. In winter it was almost impossible to sleep as the ships tossed and pitched like bucking broncos. They were more like submarines, with the sea breaking over them and we were seldom dry. Coming off watch, our eyes red and burning with lack of sleep and coal dust, we made our way down to our quarters, shed our dripping oilskins and sea boots and collapsed on our bunks in our damp clothes, too tired to bother to eat. Yet I loved the challenge those colliers gave me.

I was now past my sixteenth birthday. The year was 1939 and everyone seemed to be expecting war any day. Then, one Sunday morning as we sailed up the Clyde, the news came over the radio. We were now at war with Germany. I can remember listening to the news with a feeling of great adventure and excitement. How was I to know then, in the folly of my youth, that through the blundering of politicians and the hatred of man for his fellow man, we had just been plunged into an era of death and destruction so great that it would seem that God had turned against the very things he had created and that I, in my small way, was to witness so much of that destruction and death. I was to see and know fear in those terrible years that lay ahead.

Each time I came home I became more and more aware that my mother's health was failing fast. I pleaded with her to see a doctor, but with a smile she said, "Don't worry, son. I will be alright." Then she would, in turn, implore me to give up the sea and get a safer job on land, for I was still too young to be in the war. I replied, saying, "Surely, Mother, you do not want a coward for a son."

The war started with a few scattered air raids, confined to the south of England, and I began to wonder what all the fuss was about. The ships were all now painted in Admiralty grey, and all lights, including navigation lights, were blacked out, which added to the hazards of the sea. Guns, and trained gunners to man them, were in short supply and so I took a course in gunnery at Whitefield Road in Glasgow, and qualified as a machine gunner. I must have been one of the youngest machine gunners at that time. I found myself the only gunner on many of the ships in which I sailed in those early days, with only one gun, a Strip Lewis, on board.

I came home from one of my voyages to be told that my mother had been taken to the Southern General Hospital the previous day. I reached her bedside, but she was too ill to recognise me. The sister on the ward took me into her office and asked me what other relatives I had. When I told her I had none she seemed to be very distressed. She told me that my mother was very, very ill. I made my way back to my ship, too shocked to think clearly.

Early the following morning the Captain sent for me. He had just received word that my mother had died. He asked me if there was anyone to help me with the arrangements. When I told him there was no-one he detailed one of the able-bodied seamen to take time off to assist me. The seaman was called Archie and he was wonderful. He attended to everything. At the graveside Archie and I were the only mourners. As I turned away from that grave I felt very bitter and as if my heart must burst. Other people had homes and relatives, mothers and fathers. Why take my mother when she was all I had? There was no God. She had been wrong to tell me there was.

Archie and I returned to my mother's empty room. I sold the furniture to the landlady for five pounds and she then told me the story my mother had told her. It seemed that when my mother had come to Glasgow on the pretext of seeing me, it was really to see a specialist. He had given her two years to live, but never once had she let me know.

And so we returned to the ship just in time to sail. I was returning to the war. There was nobody now to care what happened to me and I cared least of all. What had she wanted to tell me that last day on the island? Now I would never know – or so I thought then.

Chapter Three

War Breaks Out

The air raids were now getting more frequent and greater in their intensity. Mines were being dropped around our main sea ports. Ships were being sunk at an ever increasing pace. Yes, war was becoming a very serious business indeed.

I was still sailing on those tough little colliers up and down an area called 'U-boat Alley', well known and dreaded by all coastal seamen at that time. The reason this part got its name was the fact that the Germans had small, fast torpedo submarines known as U-boats. At night, under cover of darkness, they would nip into small groups of coastal ships, torpedo one, and be off before our escorting vessels could deal with them. They played merry hell with our coastal shipping for quite a time.

During the day we had the dive bombers to contend with and of course the mines. The latter were everywhere. There were numerous types, with one of the worst being known as the magnetic mine. It lay on the seabed and as a ship passed over it, acted like a huge magnet, drawing the mine up towards the keel of the ship. It would then blow the ship to pieces.

To combat the dive bombers, we flew what were known as kites from the foremast. They were shaped like the kites with which children play, but were of course very much bigger. They were attached to a reel of fine wire and flown about a hundred and fifty feet above the ship. The idea was to keep the attacking planes as high as possible.

On one occasion we were sailing in a group of four ships when without warning, three dive bombers hurtled down out of the clouds on top of us. I raced for my machine gun post, but the second officer was already blazing away. I turned back to the kite. It was just clear of the top of the mast. The wire had jammed, preventing it from gaining height. I became engrossed in trying to free the wire and did not notice that one of the planes had decided to give our ship its undivided attention. The first thing I knew about it was the deck all around me being ploughed up by bullets. Afterwards, I measured the distance between where I had been standing and where the bullets had landed. It measured exactly four inches.

I was now approaching my eighteenth birthday, and was what was known as an Efficient Deck Hand (EDH). Although I had been at sea for almost four years and had passed my Board of Trade Certificate to sail as an Able-Bodied Seaman, the time I had spent in the catering department did not count, which meant I did not yet have enough deck service to sail as an AB. I had therefore to be content for the time being.

After days at sea, threatened by U-boats at night, dive bombers during the day, the constant possibility of being blown to bits at any moment by mines, and of course the sea itself, which has no respect for either war or peace, we would tie up in port, too exhausted even to go ashore. All we wanted was the luxury of a night's sleep, tied up in the safety of a harbour. We collapsed on our bunks, unwashed, with two or three days' beard growth on our weather-beaten faces and slipped into that unconscious paradise of sleep. But not for long; we would be woken by the scream of bombs, the crack of the Ack-Ack guns and the crunch of explosions as the bombs found their targets. Another bloody air raid. Could they not have allowed us just a few hours' sleep? And so we would leave port, sometimes having had less sleep than we got at sea. It was hard in those days to know which was worse, the land or the sea.

At night, as we sailed down the English coast, we had a grandstand view of the death and destruction taking place on land. The sky above us was filled with the roar of German bombers as they made their way to drop their cargoes of death on our towns and cities. We were helpless spectators as we watched the red glow of the fires and it seemed to us that all England was in flames.

One night, as we sailed alone and stealthy down the Bristol Channel, we heard the drone of a single German bomber making his way towards the coast. It was a very dark night and he could not see us as we had no lights. By this time we were all experts at distinguishing a loaded bomber from a light one by the drone of the engines. This one was loaded alright. As he passed over and the drone faded in the distance our captain, who was elderly but quite a character, gave the order, "Switch on all navigation lights." We were all stunned and thought that perhaps the strain of recent days had proved too much for him and he had cracked up. With all lights on we felt as if we were walking up a main street with no clothes on. The bomber turned, coming nearer and nearer and the cold, damp sweat of fear made us shiver. Death was only minutes away. Closer and closer he came. When it seemed that he was right on top of us the Captain ordered all lights off and the helm hard to port. Next thing all hell was let loose. A stick of bombs fell off our starboard side. The little ship seemed to jump clear of the sea and as she settled down again a huge column of water washed right over the bridge. We kept altering course, this way then that, with the bomber circling overhead. At last he started off back towards the coast, and again we switched on all lights. The bomber returned and dropped another lot of bombs, again just missing us. This exercise was carried out three times, after which the Captain ordered us to proceed on normal course.

"He must have killed a lot of fish tonight," he said with a chuckle. "Better that than people. I don't think he has many bombs left. Anyway, I think he will have to make for home as he has used a hell of a lot of fuel. I doubt if he will get an Iron Cross, the silly bastard."

I wondered that night if I would survive the war and someday have children. Perhaps I would watch them play hide and seek, and then I would tell them the story of the night we played it with a German bomber. Unlike that innocent child's game, if we had been caught we would certainly have been killed. This war certainly was live. The sea was our stage and we were the actors.

One day we sighted a mine and I was sent to blow it up with a burst of machine gun fire. It was one of the old type, a floating mine and it had to be struck on one of its horns in order to explode it. With everyone on board watching, I sent burst after burst of fire into that mine, but it was damned if it would blow up. I spent enough ammunition to blow up a battleship. A small naval patrol vessel came in sight, ordered us to cease fire and blew the mine up in one shot. With her Morse lamp she sent us the following message: 'Better luck next time, old chap. Try hitting the bloody mine next time and not the fish!' I got some ribbing from my mates that day, with remarks like, "You could not hit a bloody cow on the backside with a stick!" I just had to grin and bear it, but my turn was to come a few days later.

We were lying at anchor at Milford Haven, waiting to proceed down the Bristol Channel. It was just getting dark and I was on watch. A ship lying at anchor makes many queer noises, the clanking of the anchor chain for instance, but these sounds are all familiar to the experienced ear of a sailor. I thought I could hear a strange sound and decided to go forward and check the anchor chain. I looked over the starboard bow and there, to my utter horror, was a mine, not five feet off the ship's bow and dancing off the anchor chain. It was the same type as the one I had failed to blow up. I stood there as if hypnotised. I could not take my eyes off those sinister horns. Again I had that feeling of crawling fear and my throat was so dry I could not swallow. Below me were men asleep, unaware that death was only the thickness of the ship's plates away. At last my senses came back to me. I raced down and, with a hoarse voice, raised the alarm. Men tumbled out of their bunks as if they were on fire.

Soon we were all on deck, leaning over the rail. By now the mine was bouncing between the anchor chain and the ship's belting. This is a ledge which goes round the ship while in port, to protect her sides against the quay. Fortunately we were loaded, as this made the belting lie lower in the water. Had we been sailing with little cargo, the ledge would have been higher and with the slight swell of the sea, the danger was that the mine might have bounced up below the ledge, striking one of the horns. As it was, the mine was riding along the belting on its main casing, with its horns clear, but it would only take a slight alteration in the swell of the sea and the war would be over as far as we were concerned. The tension was unbearable as the mine ran down the ship's side towards the stern. I was ordered to man the machine gun, and when or if the mine cleared the stern, to open fire at a hundred and fifty yards. This was very close, but as it was getting dark and there were a lot of ships nearby at anchor that mine simply had to be exploded. This time I must not fail.

As I stood at my post I heard a great cheer from my mates. The mine had cleared the ship. I looked at the sea astern and there it was, bobbing up and down. Further and further it drifted astern. Less than half a mile away lay a large cargo ship, unaware of the danger approaching. Our Captain, on the bridge with his Aladdin lamp, sent a message across to her: 'Mine approaching you to starboard. My gunner opening fire to explode.'

I looked through the sights of the Lewis gun. The dot was getting smaller by the minute. I could not wait any longer. I remember feeling like the leading actor in a film. All eyes were on me and that bloody awful mine. I steadied my sights and pressed the trigger. Again the thought came, 'You must not fail! You must not fail!' I watched the tracers arch away towards the target. Suddenly I was blinded by a huge, orange flash, followed by a deep roar. I had exploded the mine with my first few bullets. Considering it was almost dark it certainly was a lucky shot. A great cheer went up from all my mates.

"A bloody good night's work," said Captain, who had come along to meet me, "and by the way, the Captain over there has also asked me to congratulate you on a beautiful piece of marksmanship."

As he was speaking to me, a small patrol vessel came in close to us. It was the same one that had blown up the other mine. He did not seem to recognise us, and, through a hailer, addressed our ship.

"Congratulations, Captain. Ask your gunner if he would like to transfer to the Royal Navy. We could do with some good gunners."

"Took your advice from last time, old chap," our Captain replied. "Fish in area not so good just now. Do you remember, old chap?"

"Well, well! Fancy meeting you again. Full apologies, Captain, and damned good shooting. Good luck and goodbye till we meet again."

I was the hero that night. I had been the first to spot the mine and I had proved that I could hit a cow on the backside with a stick, but I knew it had been more the luck of the game than good shooting. Still, I felt very pleased with myself. War had its compensations.

The following day we formed a small convoy and headed into the Bristol Channel. We had two escorts, one an armed trawler and the other our friend the patrol vessel, which was lying to our port side. Everything was quiet and we sailed along hour after hour. The sea began to rise, but there was no wind. Suddenly there was an orange flash to our port side, followed by that now familiar explosion. It was the patrol boat. She seemed to rise out of the water and then plunged bow first below the waves. It all happened in minutes. She had struck a mine. The other escort raced to the spot, but we later heard there were no survivors. As I looked at that empty sea I could almost hear that laughing voice saying, from the depths, "Good luck and goodbye till we meet again."

I seemed to live a charmed life in those days. On one occasion we were lying in Cardiff and across the dock lay a large cargo ship. There was the usual air raid on but the dockers had decided to carry on working. Suddenly there was an explosion. A bomb had dropped smack down into her hold, killing the dockers like rats in a trap. Another night I had been in the town of Cardiff, where I had had a few drinks, and was unaware that there was an air raid on. I was walking down Bute Road, better known to seamen as 'Tiger Bay'. I felt very hungry as I walked down the road and I remembered there was a small fish and chip shop nearby, however as I approached it an old air raid warden got hold of me.

"What are you doing – trying to commit suicide? Don't you know there is an air raid on? Come on, get into that shelter," he said, pointing to an underground shelter across from the fish shop.

"Let me get a fish supper first and then I will go into the shelter," I said, trying to reason with him. But he was adamant. We stood at the top of the flight of stairs which led down into the shelter and argued.

"You bloody old ones, give you a uniform and you're worse than Hitler!" I said. At that moment there was a huge explosion. The warden and I were picked up like paper dolls and hurled down the stairs. A landmine had landed on top of the building opposite. Now there was no building, no shop, and no fish supper for me. I owed that old warden my life but I could not thank him. He was dead, his head smashed in where he must have struck it on the stone stairway. If I had not argued with him perhaps he would still have been alive, but then the war was full of what ifs.

Another night in Bristol I was in an area known as the Old Market. There was a particularly heavy air raid that night and again I was ordered into a shelter. Sitting next to me was a huge lady, who must have weighed every bit of sixteen stones. Her bosom was in proportion to the rest of her body. As we sat in the dim light, we could hear the crunch of bombs as they exploded around us. I could smell the cold sweat of human fear, to which I had now become accustomed. As the bombs fell closer the tension was at breaking point. Then we heard the scream of one bomb coming nearer and nearer. It seemed that this one must surely plunge among us. Some prayed while others became hysterical. Suddenly I was hurled to the floor with a great weight on top of me. It was pitch dark and I was choking for air. As I struggled to free myself I thought we had had a direct hit and I was buried alive. What had really happened was that the tension had become too great for the poor lady sitting next to me. She had thrown me to the floor and she was on top of me, my head buried in her ample bosom. War certainly had its compensations.

On one of my trips home to Glasgow I learned to my great sorrow that Archie, who had looked after and comforted me at my mother's funeral, had been lost at sea. We had split up two months before when he had decided to sail on foreign going ships or 'deep sea', as we in the Merchant Navy called it. That night we had gone to a small dockside bar in Glasgow, well known to the tough seamen from the nearby ships. As we parted Archie had told me to look after myself.

"Someday you will meet a nice girl and have a home again. This war will not last for ever, you know," he had said. And now he was gone.

I decided to return to that bar and get damned drunk. I entered through the swing doors and made for the part of the bar where Archie and I had stood that night. Two men were standing on the spot, so I squeezed between them to order my drink. One of the men looked at me.

"Harry, look who we have here!" he said loudly to his mate. "It's the laddie from the croft." It was Joe and big Harry from my first ship. The two of them were now sailing together deep sea. We had a wonderful night together swapping yarns about all the things that had happened to us since we last met. I asked Joe why he had been so angry with me that night about the tin of fruit.

"Listen to me, son," he replied, "I have been stealing all my life. I am too old now to change my ways. You are young, so never start, for it never does you any good." And so we parted, more drunk than sober.

After another month on the coast I decided it was time for me to go deep sea. I reported to the Merchant Navy pool and was signed on as an AB on a Belgian tanker. At eighteen years old I was still very young to be sailing as an Able Bodied Seaman, but seamen were beginning to be in short supply, for the losses of men and ships were becoming alarming.

The tanker I joined was about ten thousand tons. All her crew were Belgian, and very few could speak any English at all. She had escaped from some port before the Germans took it, and had made a dash for Britain. We sailed down the Clyde in ballast, which meant that we had water instead of oil in our tanks, to keep the ship solid in heavy seas. I learned that we were going out to the Dutch West Indies and I wondered if I would ever see the Clyde again. In those days tankers were known as the death and glory ships of the Merchant Fleet because of the dangerous nature of their cargoes. If you were mined, torpedoed or bombed on a tanker, you went up and not down on her. The lucky ones were those who died immediately, for those who survived the initial explosion were either cremated alive or had the choice of jumping into the sea and being boiled alive in burning oil.

Hitler knew that if he could stop the supplies of oil reaching this country, victory would be his in a matter of weeks. Therefore tankers became the main targets in all convoys. Sometimes, because of the danger to other ships in the convoy, tankers were placed on the periphery, which left them very open to attack by U-boats. Sailing on a tanker was like trying to sail across the ocean on a live mine. Few indeed were the survivors from those ships.

Our voyage out was uneventful. The U-boats were happy to save the torpedoes until we were homeward bound with our precious cargoes. Then they would attack. We arrived at Port of Spain, Trinidad, and then sailed on to Aruba[1]. Then, loaded down with Benzine and a little crude oil, we started back for Freetown, West Africa, where we would pick up the main convoy for home. We had enough explosive material on board to blow up a city. How we managed to make Freetown was a miracle in itself, as we sailed alone throughout those long, long days.

As we entered the port of Freetown, a large convoy was assembling. We lay there for two days and snatched as much sleep as we could in preparation for the many sleepless days that lay ahead of us. The night before we left a naval Corvette came alongside, asking for particulars regarding our speed, destination, and the nature of our cargo. When her Captain heard we had five thousand tons of aviation spirits on board he exclaimed, "You are very brave men. May God sail with you, and we will give our lives to protect you."

---

1   Dutch Caribbean island off the coast of Venezuela. During the war the island was administered by the Dutch government in exile in London and supplied oil to Britain and her allies.

As dawn began to light the sky the ships began to raise their anchors and take up their positions. We were placed at the tail end of our column; the most dangerous position in any convoy as the U-boats used to sneak up on the rear of the convoys, picking off the stragglers. There was no alternative for us, as we were too dangerous to put anywhere else in the convoy. Had we been hit by a torpedo or bomb the explosion would have been so great that we would probably have taken other ships with us.

And so we began the long, dangerous journey home; a journey to the very gates of hell. I wondered, as I looked at the long columns of ships, how many of us would survive to sail in triumph into those far distant ports of home. And then I thought of our ship, and wondered what odds a bookmaker would give on our chances.

There were five tankers, including ourselves, in that convoy of about thirty ships altogether. We were heavily escorted by four destroyers, two of them American, sold to Britain by our allies, and two corvettes. It was a very slow convoy, sailing at seven knots. For the first few days everything was uncannily quiet, yet we had a terrible feeling that unseen eyes were watching and biding their time.

On the sixth day out from Freetown the first attack came. It was about ten o'clock at night, in that strange twilight of the tropics when it is neither dark nor light. Torpedoes streaked from port to starboard and starboard to port and ships seemed to go down all over the place. We were under a concentrated attack by at least three U-boats. It seemed that one U-boat had picked us out as its particular target. Torpedoes ran across our bow and stern, missing us by a few feet. The corvette which had spoken to us in Freetown had come in dangerously close. Suddenly she seemed to increase speed and a moment later there was the now familiar flash. She had taken a direct hit. It looked as if she had deliberately taken the torpedo heading directly for us. She keeled over and sank within minutes. Again I was to look at that empty space of sea and hear from its depths a voice saying, "We will give our lives to protect you." They were not professionals like us; the officers were probably company directors, accountants or perhaps lawyers and the youthful crew were most likely labourers or tradesmen.

We were now heading for the most dreaded part of our journey, the Bay of Biscay. If we could survive that we still had a chance to make it home. As we entered the bay all hell was let loose. Bombs rained from the sky by day, and at night the U-boats attacked in force. They were determined that none of us would ever reach England. The night was lit up like day with the glow of burning ships, and then there was darkness as they plunged below the surface. On our first night in the bay it was pretty dark, and on our starboard side was a large Norwegian tanker. Suddenly there was a flash, followed by the usual explosion. She had been hit by torpedoes.

Flames shot at least a hundred feet in the air, lighting up the whole convoy and the sea for miles around. We watched in horror and helplessness as the blazing oil gushed from her side, setting fire to the sea around her. We could see some of her crew huddled together on the only part of the ship that was not burning and others jumping into the blazing sea, to be burned alive.

One of our destroyers made a brave attempt to reach the stricken tanker, sailing through that burning sea. She made the ship's bow and the U-boats seemed to hold their fire in recognition of such bravery. The men began to jump on to the deck of the destroyer but she could wait no longer, and had to withdraw. Nothing could save those men now. To add to the horror, the wind forced the tanker to swing round and flames enveloped her, sweeping over her bow. There was a terrible explosion and then she was gone, leaving only that blazing sea.

The few survivors swam desperately for the rescue ship which was standing by outside the blaze, but the change of wind that had altered the tanker's position had also changed the direction of the fire on the sea. It followed those survivors with ruthless intent. Gathering speed, it overtook and swept over those helpless beings. The sheer horror of it all held us spellbound. Surely this was a terrible nightmare? It *was* a nightmare of damnable, bloody war, but slowly my brain began to realise I was not dreaming and once again I thought, 'how could there be a God to allow such things to happen?' I vowed that if I arrived home safely I would never sail on another tanker. But I was to sail on two more before the war was to end.

And so the battered remnants of that convoy arrived defiantly home to British waters. We had lost thirteen ships. Of the original five tankers three of us remained, which was good odds in those days, and said much for the daring of our naval escorts. Our tanker was originally intended to sail up the Manchester Canal to Manchester to discharge, but with the heavy air raids taking place, and with our deadly cargo, the risk was too great. Instead we were put into a remote part of Liverpool Bay, while the top brass decided what to do with us.

Our problems however, were still not over. We lay there for four days. During the day we stood on deck and watched the dog-fights between the German fighter planes and our own taking place above us. At night, during the heavy raids, we listened to the gentle swoosh of the mines as they were dropped in the sea around us. At last, with the minesweepers sweeping a channel in front of us, we made our way up the canal to Ellesmere Port. We had made it home when so many had not. It was with a feeling of great satisfaction that I was paid off that ship. We had brought home enough fuel to keep our young fighter pilots happy for quite a time to come.

And so, with a week's leave due to me and a good bundle of notes in my pocket, I bade my Belgian mates farewell. They had been a great bunch of chaps but I had been very lonely on that voyage, for I could not speak their language and they could not speak English. I booked into a first class hotel in Lime Street and lived like a king with wine, women and song. Before long I was broke and I reported back for duty before my leave was up.

I sailed again to Velva in Spain, then to Gibraltar, this time on a small, general cargo ship. At least this time there was a better chance I would make it. Heading home again across the bay was a replica of the previous trip, with ships to port, starboard, ahead and astern blazing, exploding and sinking. Again we made it and tied up in the East India Docks in London. With a few pounds in my pocket and a few days leave, I decided to head for Glasgow.

As soon as I arrived I made for the Merchant Navy pool office. I knew I would meet some of my old shipmates around there and get all the news. Sure enough, I met a chap called Kenny who had sailed on my first ship as an ordinary seaman when I was galley boy. We were delighted to see each other and adjourned to a nearby bar to swap yarns about our experiences since those peacetime days when we had sailed together. How long ago it seemed. I asked him if he was still going with the same girl called Jessie, whom I had met on a couple of occasions, and he told me he was. I then told him of my chance meeting with Big Harry and Joe, and wondered if I might see them down at the pool. I was shocked to hear that they had both been lost at sea two months before.

Up till now I had been extremely fortunate. In most ships in which I had sailed I was the only member who had not been torpedoed at least once, but I had a terrible premonition that my next trip was going to prove different. With that uneasy feeling in mind I decided to visit my mother's grave the following day. In the meantime I would visit that small, dockside bar again.

I entered the swinging doors and made my way to that same spot at the bar. The place was full of the men I had come to know so well, with their blue sailor's jerseys, their light blue dungarees and jackets, their already tanned faces more flushed than ever as they threw back the raw whisky and ordered more. They slapped each other on the back and roared with laughter, probably at some dirty joke. Others looking in that door would have turned up their noses at those tough looking men. How wrong they would have been. I knew those men. I had seen them fight and I had seen them die a thousand deaths. I thought of Joe and I thought of Harry, and as I downed my drink, I remembered Joe's words that night, "I have been stealing all my life. Don't start, son. It never does you any good."

Next day I stood alone beside my mother's grave and the memories of her flooded my mind. I looked at the spot where Archie had stood that day and I thought of the last time we had met and his words to me, "Remember this war will not last forever." All the pent-up tension, the memories of all the Joes, Harrys and Archies, the terrible feelings of loss for my mother and of being alone exploded inside me and hot, bitter tears rolled down my cheeks. In those last two years I had often felt fear but I had always controlled it; those tears I could not. As I turned away from the graveside to join my next ship, I had a feeling that wherever my mother's soul might be, it might not be long until I joined her. I knew that my next trip would tell and I was not to be proved wrong.

Chapter Four

Shipwreck

When I entered the pool office the following morning I still had two days leave left, but I felt fed up hanging around, for I had never become accustomed to cities, with their grey buildings and hard pavements. Though life at sea was hell, I loved the feeling of a ship's deck heaving under my feet.

It was now the end of June, 1942. The battle of the Atlantic seemed to have reached its full, relentless fury. At times it seemed as if we must lose the battle. In fact I believed we were a matter of weeks from surrender. No nation could stand this appalling loss of ships and men and hope to survive. It certainly looked as if we, like all those other countries before us, were about to fall prey to the might of the Germans. The world watched in awe as the greatest battle ever to be waged on the oceans of the world swayed this way and that. The occupied countries looked on with trembling fear. How could they be freed if we lost this battle? It was now up to us, the Merchant seamen, along with our young and daring partners, the Royal Navy escorts, to prove that Britannia still ruled the waves, and no matter the sacrifice, we would continue until every U-boat was blasted from the depths of the seas, or until we had no seamen or ships left to fight.

Those, then, were the hazards I knew I faced as the pool's officer told me to report to Oban. I knew there was a large convoy forming off Greenock, and I asked the pool's officer why I could not get a ship there, instead of going to Oban.

"If it were me, son," he replied with a wink, "I would go to Oban." I realised then that the convoy at Greenock must be Russia bound, and as I did not want to be a dead hero, went to Oban.

I put up for the night in a Merchant Navy hostel in Oban, with instructions to be at the Merchant Navy office at ten the next morning to be signed on. It turned out that I was the replacement for a seaman who had been taken ashore with appendicitis. How I was to curse that appendix in the coming weeks.

I entered the office and stated my business. A medium built man of about five feet ten, wearing four gold rings, came forward and introduced himself as the captain of the ship I was about to join. He looked to me to be a man in his fifties. After the formalities of signing on, he told me the ship was lying in Loch Ewe and as he had more business to attend to he would meet me at the jetty at four that afternoon. We would then get the liberty boat out to the ship. I asked him for a 'sub', which was an advance on my wages and he gave me three pounds. I made my way towards the nearest bar and ordered a drink and I thought of that captain. He seemed very abrupt and severe and yet there was a quality about him I liked. Little did I know then how much I was to owe to this man.

As I waited that day I speculated as to which part of the world I would sail to on this voyage, and what kind of ship it would be. I still had the uneasy feeling of impending disaster. But as the drink took effect I began not to care whether I came back or not. After all, I told myself, there is nobody to mourn me anyway. That made me feel worse. It seems a strange quirk of human nature that people do like to be missed and mourned.

The liberty boat headed out of Oban Bay, rounded a point of land and there, lying before us, was a large convoy, made up of all shapes and sizes of ships riding their anchors. As we chugged our way between them, I wondered how many would be lying at the bottom of the ocean in a few weeks' time. We started heading for the oldest, rustiest looking tramp steamer[2] I had ever seen outside a ship-breaker's yard. She looked

2 A tramp steamer operates with no fixed schedule or published ports of call. The tramp is a descendant of the early merchant ships whose masters (who were also their owners) loaded them with cargo at home to sell abroad, and vice versa. Tramps are used mainly for carrying bulk commodities or homogeneous cargoes in whole shiploads, with each voyage separately negotiated between the ship's owner and the shipper, usually through a broker.

as if she had lain at the bottom of the ocean for years and then been salvaged and put straight into service. This, then, was to be my new home.

Once I had clambered up the rope ladder which dangled from her rusty side, and stepped on to her deck, I realised that the view from outside paid her credit, for she looked a damned sight worse inside. She had probably been laid up waiting to be scrapped, but now anything that could float and carry cargo had to be used. I looked up at her bridge. She had no wheelhouse, just a canvas dodger round the bridge. The crew's quarters were up in the bow, known as the foc'sle; the sailors' on the port side and the firemen on the starboard side. The firemen were all West African. There was a communal toilet consisting of two lone troughs facing each other, one for the firemen and one for the sailors. When nature called each trough would sit four men. At a full house, it was like sitting in the Glasgow subway, gazing across at your partner in the opposite seat. There was certainly no racial discrimination on this ship, and even less privacy. Along one wall of the toilet there was a board with about six round holes cut in it. I was later to discover that each man had a galvanized bucket, which he took along midships. He would fill it with cold water then take it back and place it in one of the holes. That was how we washed. Some buckets had a red lead cross on them, which meant the owner had picked up a well-known disease, so no one else would use his pail.

This was certainly going to be a tough trip, even without assistance from the Germans. But these things apart, she was one of the cleanest tramp steamers I ever sailed on, and her engine room was a credit to her engineers. Never have I seen an engine room gleam like it did on that old tramp, not even on passenger ships. As a general cargo tramp steamer she was small, about four thousand tons. Apart from the chief engineer I was the only Scotsman on board, the rest of the officers, deck crew and catering staff being English.

At eleven-thirty that night I was ordered to the chain locker, as we were heaving up the anchor. This was a back-breaking job that nobody liked. I went down the iron ladder into a chamber about twenty feet square and about fifteen feet deep and as the winch on deck pulled the anchor from the sea bed, the chain came up into the chamber through a hole called the hosepipe. My job was to spread the chain evenly back and forth across the chamber. The chain was, of course, dripping wet, and the links very heavy. It was not so bad when the chamber was almost empty, but as the anchor came nearer the surface, the locker became more and more full, until I was bringing in the last few fathoms almost bent in two. Moreover, if the chain happened to slip off the windlass above, the chain in the chamber would fly back out of the hosepipe, taking what was left of me with it to the bottom of the sea. It had been known to happen so the thought was always there. Even in those days most ships had self-stowing chain lockers, thus doing away with this backbreaking job.

My task completed, I came up on deck and saw the ships take up their stations in the familiar long columns of a sea-going convoy. I watched the escort destroyers and corvettes as they fussed about their flock. They always reminded me of the sheepdogs at home as they rounded up the sheep. Thinking of home, I looked over to our starboard beam. About thirty-five miles away lay my little island, so near and yet so far. I sometimes wondered if I would ever see it again, but that night I was very sure I would not. And so we headed well out to sea and down towards the South Atlantic.

The first three days were pretty stormy, with rough head seas running, and it was damned cold on that open bridge, especially when we had to do two hours of our four hour watches at the helm. Like the rest of the ship, her steering left much to be desired. It was the old chain driven system and we carried a half turn of port or starboard helm all the time, to try to keep her in line with the ship ahead. It was like driving a car and having to turn the steering wheel a full turn before the car would start to answer the wheel. Being at the helm was like trying to sit on a bucking bronco. There were no mod cons on this old lady and I became convinced that she had been converted from sail to steam.

The convoy itself consisted of thirty-five ships and I was surprised to find that we did not have a big escort. Probably there was some very good reason for this, but I had sailed on smaller convoys with a much heavier escort. By this time I knew where we were going. It seemed that we were making for the River Plate[3], calling at Montevideo, Santos and Buenos Aires and it would be a voyage of about four months. I was glad to hear this news on two counts; firstly because we would be in the tropics most of the time so the open bridge would not be so cold and secondly, being a young sailor, I had heard all about the nightlife in those ports. Deep down though, I knew that one way or the other none of us was destined to see any of those places, not on this trip at any rate.

There was one AB on board to whom I had taken a great liking and it seemed the feeling was mutual. His name was Jack and he had sailed on trawlers all his life. His favourite saying was that one was not a sailor until one had sailed on a trawler. He had joined the Merchant Navy at the outbreak of the war and had already been torpedoed twice. He was a man in his middle forties, about five feet nine and very thin with a bald head and he was as tough as nails. Like most sailors though, he was very superstitious.

One day the two of us were sitting on number two hatch when a rat appeared.

"Jock," said Jack, addressing me, "take a word of advice from one who knows. Keep your life jacket on. Never let it out of your sight, for this old tub will never see the Plate. I can feel it in my bones. And when she gets hit, it will be smack in the middle of this hold we are sitting on. Rats always know." I dismissed the part about the rats as being the thoughts of a superstitious old fisherman, but the rest of his statement made my throat go dry, for they were exactly my sentiments.

The food on board was the usual fare that one would expect to find on the average ship, no better, no worse, but one day we were served stew which I did not think was good enough. I was not backward at any time in expressing my opinion to those responsible, even if it were the Captain himself. I made straight for the Chief Steward's cabin and gave him a piece of my mind. I demanded to know if that was what was being

---

3   Rio de la Plata, a large estuary between Argentina and Uruguay.

served to the officers. I finished by telling him that if we were given any more of that garbage during the remainder of the voyage, I would report him to my union when we got back to Britain.

The convoy steamed on into the South Atlantic and each day the weather improved, getting warmer the further south we went. There were no alerts or incidents of any kind, however now and again one of the escorts would drop depth charges at the rear of the convoy. This was not normal practice unless they had reason to suspect we were being followed. I most certainly felt we were. Something else which had me wondering was the fact that, unlike other convoys which usually sailed light on the outward journey, this one was loaded. Why then were the U-boats not attacking? After all they could win both ways. Even if they sank the exports and ships on the way out, the remainder of the ships still had to return home with their precious cargoes, so, either way, they must win. There seemed something eerie and sinister about this convoy that I could not explain.

On our tenth day out, at ten in the morning, the alarm went. Unidentified aircraft approaching. Usually when the alarm went I had that sinking feeling in my stomach. It always reminded me of the sensation I had when I was a small boy, an hour after my mother had given me my weekly dose of castor oil. It was with a feeling of relief that I donned my steel helmet and strapped myself into the twin Hotchkiss machine gun. Maybe at last we were going to see action. It would at least be better than the uneasy silence. As I scanned the clear sky I could hear the drone of a plane. Following the sound, I spotted him. He was flying across the convoy, well out of the range of our guns. At that height, it was hard to identify what he was, but to me he looked like a Focke-Wulf 200. This was a four engined, long range German Bomber.

After the alarm was over I clambered down from the gun pit, and met Jack.

"Well, son, just you remember to keep that life jacket on. Make sure your sheath knife is on your belt and carry plenty of cigarettes with you, for that plane was spotting for the subs. Every bleeding U-boat in the area will know our position."

That night we expected the U-boats to attack, but nothing happened. At three in the afternoon of the following day five ships, including ourselves, were told to leave the convoy and head for our destinations together. We assumed the other four were also heading for the Plate. Our blood ran cold as we watched the main convoy disappear over the horizon. Here we were, five of us, with no escort detailed to look after us, heading down the Azores, known to every seaman as the graveyard of ships. At that time our planes did not have the range to patrol this area, so it was known also as the playground of the U-boats. They hunted in packs, just like wolves, sometimes not even bothering to submerge. We all knew then that our fates were sealed and that it would only be a matter of time.

The five of us formed into a group: two ships ahead of us, one off our port bow, the other off the starboard; two astern, one on the starboard quarter and the other on the port. They were about a mile ahead and the same astern. As darkness fell I made sure my sheath knife was on my belt. I stuck two boxes of fifty cigarettes in my pocket. I then got out the only photos I had of my mother and some other papers, including a Post Office bank book with around twenty pounds in it. I stuck them all into a canvas bag and strapped it to a belt around my waist. It was a dark night, but very clear. A fresh wind was blowing but that was to be expected, for we were now in the trade winds and the sea had a moderate swell. I was off watch until midnight, when the first two hours of my watch would be on standby duty and my second two hours would be at the helm. But though I was off watch, like the rest of the crew, there was no sleep for me.

At ten that night there was a brilliant flash, followed by an explosion off our port bow. Minutes later there was another explosion on the starboard bow. The two ships ahead had been torpedoed. We about turned and headed back the way we had come. The two ships which had been astern of us had done likewise. By the time I went on watch at midnight, one of them had also been hit, and, by one in the morning, the second. Again we doubled back on our original course, and zigzagged and raced for our lives. Later we were told we had been doing all of twelve knots. We would never have believed the old lady had it in her. She was straining and shuddering in every rivet. The tension on board was at breaking point. We were in the middle of a pack of U-boats, like a mouse surrounded by cats and we had no chance.

At one forty-five I decided to go into the galley for a smoke, before taking over the helm at two. As I sat in the dimly lit galley, listening to the urgent throb of the engines and feeling the tremble and shudder as the old lady cleft the waves, I wondered when it would come and where it would strike. Suddenly, the ship's ginger cat sprang across the galley, tail straight out, fur standing on end. It seemed to sense the danger. This incident gave me quite a start, and I thought about where I was sitting, right above the furnaces. If we were hit at that moment the deck might cave in and I would find myself in hell a bit before I was due. With a shudder at the thought I left the galley in a hurry. There were only minutes left until I took over the helm. I leaned over the rail and looked across the dark sea into the night. I could almost feel those unseen eyes watching us. The wash from our bow and the wake trailing far behind the ship were gleaming white in the darkness, for the waters in the South Atlantic are full of phosphorus, which shines in the dark. Our wake would be visible from quite a distance away, thus giving away our position.

I climbed up the companion way to the bridge, tightening the cords on my life jacket, and checking my sheath knife and canvas bag. As I took over the helm the officer of the watch gave me a zigzag course. I pulled the hood of my duffle coat tighter around my ears.

"I am going below to have another check on the charts," said the Captain to the officer. "If we can keep her afloat until daylight we might be able to pick up some of those poor devils in the morning." He was referring to the survivors from the other ships. I peered down at the shrouded clock, with its small blue light. The time was five minutes past two. I looked ahead over the canvas dodger. The bow was rising, soon to crash down into the oncoming wave. It was going to be a long two hours.

Seconds later a scream from the port wing of the bridge rose above the sounds of the wind and the sea. It came from the man on lookout.

There was a blinding flash, followed by a loud explosion. The ship reared out of the water and then settled down in the sea, listing violently to port. It appeared, at that moment in time, as if she was going to turn right over. I had been thrown into the starboard wing of the bridge. It seemed all hell had been let loose; the huge jumbo derrick had crashed down onto the bridge, across the helm where I had been standing. The whole ship seemed to be falling about me. I had only one thought, which was to get off that bridge and into one of the lifeboats as soon as possible. Below me, I could hear men cursing and screaming as they struggled to lower the two lifeboats on the port side. As I fought my way under and over all kinds of obstacles, the ship was rocked by another explosion. The boilers had exploded and there was steam blowing everywhere. To add to this, the ship was on fire in the No.1 hold, and gradually listing more and more.

When, at last I made the boat deck the picture before me was like a scene from a film, only this was reality. There was a ghostly light from the flames, steam blowing just like mist on a mountain, men running back and forward not really knowing what to do and of course, everybody was shouting orders. Already one lifeboat was full and pulling away from the ship's side. I looked over the side, down at the other boat. It was almost full. The Jacob's ladder which dangled down the ship's side was still full of men, so I grabbed one of the lifelines, shut my eyes and slid down into the heaving lifeboat, fifteen feet below.

The lifeboat was now full. I looked up at the towering monster of the ship above us. It seemed as if, at any moment, she would roll right over on top of us, all four thousand tons of her, sending us all to the bottom of the sea. There was one Royal Navy gunner still clinging to the rope ladder. He had come down so far but he was frightened to come any further in case he was crushed when the lifeboat rose up the ship's side with the swell. As we rode up we shouted to him to let go, and let himself drop into the boat, but fear does many things to a man. He was petrified and glued to that ladder. It was probably his first trip to sea as a DEMS gunner and he was not yet twenty-one. As we were still attached to the ship by ropes known as painters, every second was a matter of life or death to us, for the ship could go at any minute. Therefore, with self-preservation uppermost in my mind, I readied myself and as we rose I grabbed the gunner's bell bottom trousers, shouting to him to let go. He waited too long however and the lifeboat dropped down about fifteen feet, leaving me in mid-air, clinging to the bell bottoms. As the boat started to rise towards us, the gunner let go. The two of us were hurled about twelve feet down to the boat. The gunner landed in the lifeboat, but I missed and landed in the sea, fortunately on the side furthest from the ship. Had I dropped between the ship's side and the lifeboat, I would have been pulped to mincemeat. I had hardly hit the water before I was grabbed and hauled back into the boat.

At last the order was given to chop the ropes. We drifted clear of the ship, got out the oars, and pulled hard to get as far away as possible before the boat sank. As we drew round her stern I looked up at that twelve pounder gun, useless on her poop deck. The night grew darker as we drew further away from the ship and suddenly, like some great, sinister monster from the deep, a huge black shape bore down upon us. It was the U-boat which had torpedoed us.

"God, no, he is going to ram us!" somebody screamed. I think everybody closed their eyes and prayed, waiting for the terrible impact that would mean death to us all. The seconds ticked past like hours. Above the mutterings and wailings of prayer I could hear the sound of his diesel engines come nearer and nearer. They reached us at last and I could contain myself no longer. If I were to die, I must at least have one last glimpse of life. I looked up and my heart gave a leap of joy. The long, cigar shape of the U-boat was sailing past us, about ten yards away. I remember shouting that we were saved, we were saved, and a great cheer went up. He had seen us and altered course to avoid us. He may have been a German, but he was no Nazi. The brotherhood of the sea had won.

In the distance we could see the faint glow of the fire on our ship, which meant she was still afloat. She had certainly belied her appearance and was indeed a tough old lady. Suddenly there was a flash, and a shell screamed over our heads. The U-boat was shelling the ship to make sure she sank. I thought again of that useless gun, sitting unmanned on the poop deck. After about five minutes the shelling ceased. The glow of the fire had disappeared and the ship was gone. We were alone on a dark and angry sea.

Chapter Five

Hard Decisions

As the shock of the past hour started to wear off, we began to take stock of ourselves. Firstly, there were rats everywhere, jumping all over us. We just grabbed them and flung them over the side; after all, there was little enough room as it was.

The lifeboat itself was made of wood and was twenty-two feet in length and about five feet in width. It should have had a maximum of twenty passengers, but we had twenty-eight on board, which meant that we were grossly overcrowded and to make matters worse the boat was leaking like a sieve. If we had not started bailing immediately the boat would have submerged beneath us; even despite our bailing the water was two feet deep. By a piece of good fortune we not only had the Captain with us but also a small wireless transmitter with a radius of seventy miles, which was battery operated. We could send out messages but we could not receive them, so we could not tell whether or not our messages were being received.

Our first thought was to rig up the mast, get our aerial up and start sending out our distress signal, but the Captain decided against this. He explained that the submarine must still be very close by, and if we started to send out signals the U-boat would pick them up too. We would be giving her position away as well, and she might just decide to silence us. As we were in no position to bargain we decided we would wait an hour or so, to let her get clear. They had given us our chance. We might not get another one.

We knew the other lifeboat was somewhere nearby so it was decided to put out our sea anchor, in order that we would not drift too far. The sea anchor consisted of a cone shaped piece of canvas which floated on the surface. It had two purposes: one, to stop the boat from drifting, and the second to hold the boat's head into the oncoming seas.

As dawn streaked across the sky and it got lighter, we looked around at each other. We certainly were a very sorry looking lot. Our faces were dirty and our eyes were staring, with a rather crazy look about them. It was a mixture of shock and fear. Many had their clothes in shreds, where the blast had almost ripped them from their bodies. The duffle coat and life jacket I had been wearing were gone, as was the canvas bag with the photos I treasured so much. We were all shaking violently with a mixture of cold and shock. In my case it was mostly with cold, for I was soaking from my dip in the sea. Unfortunately my cigarettes had also gone with the duffle coat.

As dawn gave way to daylight we sighted the other boat riding the swell. She was about four hundred yards off our starboard side. We hauled in our sea anchor and drew to within hailing distance of her. The Captain began to shout over to her, but the wind made it very difficult for us to hear the replies. We started a roll call among us to find out how many had been lost on the ship. At the time I understood that I was the only one to come off the bridge alive. It was not until more than twenty years later that I was to learn that no-one had been lost at all.

It was now 6 am, so we rigged up our mast and aerial and started to send out distress signals. After this was done we all felt much better. I already had visions of a sleek destroyer appearing and taking me on board to down plenty of Navy rum. How wrong that vision proved to be.

We had to remain in our present position until twelve noon, to give any ship which might have picked up our message a chance to reach us. After all, we were in quite a busy shipping area, as the U-boats knew only too well. The Captain however, had already laid his plans in the event of our not being picked up, and so he related them to us.

The nearest land to us was the Canary Islands, which lay three hundred miles to the west, however we could not attempt to sail there as the trade winds would be against us all the way. The next point of land lay seven hundred miles away, at the Cape Verde Islands[4] off the West African coast and this was where we would make for. The Captain, seeing the looks of despair on our faces, assured us we did not have to worry. We would have the trade winds with us all the way and as we would be crossing the main convoy routes, we would almost certainly be picked up. We then relayed our plans to the other boat and it was decided that both boats would set sail together at noon.

We were more overcrowded than the other boat and had only four actual sailors, the rest being the African firemen and greasers, the cook, chief steward, assistant steward, galley boy, wireless operator, chief engineer and the third officer. We therefore decided to draw alongside the other boat and even things up a bit. The sea however was rising so we had to abandon the idea as being too dangerous to attempt. If the two boats smashed together we would all be finished.

As we waited for noon, hoping all the time to be picked up, we took stock of our supplies. We had two small barrels of fresh water, which was very little between us. We had plenty of hard ship's biscuits and stuff called 'Pemmican', which was supposed to be rich in vitamins. We spread it on the biscuits like butter. We also had packets of chewing gum which one chewed to keep the saliva in one's mouth when thirst set in, but we prayed we would not have to use it.

The Captain had managed to grab his sextant before leaving the ship. This instrument was essential for navigating the boat. Each day at midday the Captain took a reading from the sun through the sextant, thus ascertaining our position. One of the officers had a waterproof watch, and with these two instruments and his experience of the sea the Captain had to navigate us across those hundreds of miles of windswept sea. One slight error of judgement on his part and we would all die a terrible death.

It was now midday. No ship had appeared so we decided to hoist our red sail and head for the Cape Verde islands seven hundred miles away.

---

4 The Cape Verde archipelago is located in the Atlantic Ocean, approximately 350 miles off the western coast of the African continent, near Senegal, The Gambia, and Mauritania.

The other boat did likewise. Again we felt the need for more experienced seamen in our boat as we struggled to get the sail up. For me there was one consolation; my old friend Jack was with us and he was a first class seaman.

The other boat was already underway. She tacked in as close as she could to us, and we shouted words of encouragement across to each other. One of the cracks was that whoever arrived first had to leave some beer and women for their mates. The other boat's sail billowed in the wind as she started to gather speed, and gradually she left us further and further behind. At last all we could see of her was the tip of her sail as she disappeared over the horizon. She had a much better chance of making it than we had.

That night we settled down to our first meal, which for most of us it was our first for almost twenty hours. It consisted of three ounces of water, one hard biscuit with Pemmican, and a piece of chewing gum. Those who had some dry cigarettes shared them out, but I doubt if there were fifty cigarettes among the lot of us. Those who had dry ones had put them, along with their matches, into rubber sheaths. When those sheaths were manufactured I am sure nobody in their wildest dreams could have thought of them being used for the purpose of keeping cigarettes and matches dry.

After our meal we tried to make ourselves as comfortable as possible, but the boat was still leaking and it was hard to find any comfort with one's feet dangling in the cold seawater and no shelter from the biting wind, as well as having wet and torn clothes. Darkness was falling and the sea was rising as we joined the Captain in prayer.

"Please, God, have mercy upon us. Give us the courage and endurance to face the difficult days that lie ahead." Above the howl of the wind the words seemed to float from the sea and the Captain's voice trailed away. Our position seemed hopeless. None of us had any experience of sailing a small boat, particularly a badly leaking and overcrowded one, with seven hundred miles of empty sea ahead.

Darkness was now fully upon us. Suddenly I felt fear as I had never known it before. For the first time since I had lost my mother I prayed. I had just passed my nineteenth birthday, and I felt I was too young to die.

Chapter Six

Battle for Survival

As the darkness of our first night gave way to the dawn of our second day we looked even more miserable than we had the previous morning. The severe cold of the night had made sleep impossible and as the boat tossed and pitched we were all violently seasick, for though we were all seasoned seamen, we were not used to this type of turbulent and unpredictable motion. Our limbs were locked with cramp and it was impossible to lie down. As it was, we were almost sitting on top of each other. Gradually a great red ball began to appear over the horizon. It was with a feeling of great relief that we began to feel the heat penetrate our frozen bodies. Even at that very early hour of the morning the sun was very warm.

As the morning wore on the Captain made further plans. First we would trim the boat, which meant shifting people about according to their weight. The idea was to get the boat as well balanced as possible so that she would ride the seas better and give all possible speed for, as we had no engine, our lives depended completely on the trade winds, our sail, and above all on the skill of our Captain's navigation.

The Captain had managed to shift the twelve African firemen so that they were all together. This was a good idea as it enabled them to talk to each other in their native tongue. The four of us who were sailors were placed at the stern, next to the Captain. This was so that we were beside the tiller, which was used for steering the boat on course. This had to be manned twenty-four hours a day, so the four of us, as the only ones with any knowledge of steering, had to take it in turn, along with the Captain. Once we were given our positions we were not allowed to change them unless the Captain ordered us to do so.

The other thing which had to be organised was the rations. The Captain had already worked out the water supply and had decided that for the time being we would have two meals a day, consisting of one biscuit with Pemmican, one piece of chewing gum and two ounces of water. The morning meal would be given out at 9 am, and the evening meal at 8 pm, before prayers.

Up until now everyone had been taking turns at bailing out. There was a hand pump fixed in the boat but it would not operate, so the chief engineer investigated and found a dead rat jammed in the inlet pipe. Once this was removed we set up a system of pumping, with each man taking a twenty minute spell. The four of us sailors and the Captain were excluded from this duty, as we were already taking turns on the tiller and were also having to reef the sail according to the winds and the Captain wanted as little movement about the boat as possible.

As the morning wore on that great red ball of sun rose higher in the clear blue, cloudless sky. Vapour rose from our bodies as our damp rags began to dry out. Pangs of hunger started to gnaw at our stomachs, and our throats felt like sandpaper. The hunger I could stand; I had experienced that feeling many times as a boy, but this feeling of thirst was new to me. At last it was time for our morning meal. The chief engineer, assisted by the chief steward, handed out the biscuit and chewing gum. The water ration was doled out in a measure made for the purpose by the Captain. It was no more than a swallow, and did little to ease the pangs of thirst.

After our meal we looked out half a dozen blankets and spread them across us to dry. We then shared the remaining cigarettes among us. One of the Africans had a large tobacco leaf, which was also spread out to dry. Another African had an old clay pipe so, the Africans being willing to share, we would have a smoke with our evening meal for a couple of nights.

It was now midday and that fiery red ball, like a demon from hell, blazed mercilessly down on our bare heads. We kept cool by leaning over the side of the boat and plunging our heads into the beautifully clear pure sea. It was a terrible temptation to open one's mouth and drink from its depths, but we had all heard too much about seamen drinking salt water and then going insane with the raging thirst which followed. Many of them committed suicide by jumping over the side into the sea. As the day wore on we prayed for the coolness of the night to come.

And so the hours passed, each one as long as a day, until that blazing hell disappeared over the rim of the horizon. It was becoming cooler and darker. It was now time for our evening meal and that wonderful sip of the most precious thing known to man – water.

After our meal we rolled up part of the dried tobacco leaf, put it into an old stained clay pipe and lit up. Each man was allowed two draws. As the tobacco and the pipe belonged to the Africans, they smoked first, then passed it around until everyone had had their ration, the Captain being the last to get his. This simple operation of smoking an African's pipe taught me a lesson that I have carried with me all my life. Here in this small boat, with death as our constant companion, there was neither racial discrimination nor class distinction. We were just human beings with a common purpose; to survive. I vowed that night that if I did survive, I would treat all men, regardless of their colour, their station in life or their beliefs, just as human beings, no more, no less.

We were now into our third day and the feeling of thirst was getting worse. I had never steered a boat before and found it very difficult at first. Although we had a small compass which we held between our knees, the boat pitched and tossed and the dial swung all over the place. At night it was much easier. One could check one's course on the compass and line a star up with the top of the mast so that, for most of the night, one steered by the star, checking now and again with the compass. As we became more used to steering, we could almost judge our course by the billow of the sail.

Our horizon, this being the distance we could see around us, was about two miles. This was because we lay so low in the water. As we rose on top of a wave we scanned the sea around us, hoping to see some sign of a ship, but all we saw was a heaving mass of blue water. We were entirely alone, without even a sign of a seabird.

Even in this position there were moments of humour. Shock does strange things to the human body and for the first two days most of us found that our bladders would not function. It was suggested that by pouring seawater down inside our trousers, the cold water would shock our bladders back to normal. Whether this helped or not the condition righted itself, but the pain was excruciating while it lasted and our cure was certainly not very comfortable. Later on in the voyage our bladders ceased to function again, but that was because there was simply no liquid left in our bodies.

Another incident occurred which involved the cook, a man who weighed around fourteen stones. There was a small area behind the sail, just big enough to enable one to stand up in the bow. As the cook was needing to fulfil one of the functions of nature, he made his way up behind the sail to get some privacy, but he did not realise that we could all see below the sail. As he bent down, with his back end over the side of the boat, the boom sail swung inboard, caught him full on his bare backside, and knocked him clean over the side. By good luck we managed to grab him and haul him back on board. Had this happened later he would have been lost, for then we had not the strength to pull him in.

About 3 pm on the third day the wind dropped slightly and the sea became a sheet of glass, with the sun kissing its surface, making it sparkle and glitter like a million jewels. I was trailing my hand in the water to keep cool and gazing ahead over the shimmering sea. Suddenly I saw three objects coming toward us. As they drew closer I realised, with a feeling of horror, that they were the huge fins of sharks. They moved in closer and passed us, then suddenly swung around and followed the boat about twenty feet astern. We were no longer alone. I wondered what would happen if they decided to attack the boat. That night, as darkness fell, we joined the Captain in prayer.

"Oh God, have mercy on us. Protect us from the perils which we face." The Captain's voice trailed away in the rising wind. I looked over his shoulder at those sinister fins, which were now only feet away from the stern, and I wondered what size were the monsters below them.

And so we settled down for our third night. It was freezing cold so we wrapped our arms around each other like lovers, the heat from our bodies keeping each other warm.

On our fifth day the Captain reckoned that we should start crossing the main convoy routes the following day, so there was every possibility that we would be sighted and picked up within the next two days. We had not sent out any more messages on our transmitter in order to preserve our battery until we reached the main shipping routes. In preparation for the following day the wireless operator hit on a plan to give the radio more power.

On each life-jacket was a small red light, clipped to the shoulder and operated by a battery. If one was floating in the sea the light came on automatically, making it easier for searching ships to see one in the dark. The operator's plan was to wire all these batteries together and then join them to the transmitter battery, thus boosting our transmitting distance by perhaps another twenty miles.

We were all beginning to look like a really wild bunch. Our beards were getting longer and the skin on our faces was peeling badly with the scorching sun, the wind and the salt water. Old Jack was certainly living up to his motto that one was not a sailor until one had sailed on a trawler. He was as tough as nails. His bald head had about two layers of burnt skin on top, but he was always cheerful and optimistic.

"How would a big mug of tea do now, Jock?" he would say to me when the sun was at its hottest. He gave me the impression that if any of us would survive, it would certainly be Jack.

While we were still on the ship, Jack had told me a story about the Captain. On the day Jack had joined the ship he had come out of the pool office with his kitbag and was looking for a taxi to take him down to the ship. By luck there was one just about to move off from the pavement. Jack ran forward and there, sitting in the taxi, was the Captain, also going to the ship.

"Excuse me, sir. May I share your taxi?" asked Jack.

"No, you cannot. There are plenty of other taxis," replied the Captain, and he drove away.

On the fourth day in the lifeboat Jack had turned to the Captain and said with a grin, "Well, we are all in the same bloody taxi now, Captain."

"Yes and I don't think there are many more about. Do you?" replied the Captain, also grinning.

The sixth day dawned, and we had now reached the convoy routes. Perhaps we were over optimistic as we all seemed to think we would see huge convoys all over the place, but as with all the other days there was nothing visible but sea. At last we started to send out our signals. Surely there were ships close enough to receive our message? It would only be a matter of time until we were picked up.

The day passed and still there was no sign of anything except those fins, following us. The seventh day followed, with the same result. Our spirits dropped. We had been so sure that we would be picked up. We were now past the convoy routes so all that lay ahead now was the Cape Verde islands and if we missed them, the coast of Africa. But we must hit those islands, for to go beyond them was unthinkable. We would be doomed to die from thirst, surely the most terrible death of all.

That night we took stock of our rations. There were plenty of biscuits but most of us had given up eating them, for they seemed to make us even more thirsty. In any case our throats were too dry and sore to swallow them. The water situation was bad and so it was decided to stop the morning ration which meant that all we would get was two ounces each night. Things were bad enough with four ounces. What was it going to be like with only two ounces every twenty four hours?

The eighth day was now upon us and still there was nothing but those three fins. Looking round the boat I could see that for many, the strain was beginning to tell. They sat there, hunched up and listless. I was still in a reasonable condition. I was young and my earlier days of privation were now standing me in good stead.

One of the sharks decided to take a closer look at us and came right alongside the boat. I could have put my hand out and stroked the fin. As we looked over the side into the clear, blue water, we could see its long body. I would have sworn it was as long as the boat. We all shuddered with horror and fear. The Captain ordered us to stop trailing our hands in the water, but he need not have.

As the ninth day dawned, the seas began to rise. The wind also rose, whipping the sea into a frenzy. Within an hour we were in the middle of a raging storm. The seas were running twenty to twenty-five feet high. The sensation we had, as we rode those waves, was like being on the Big Dipper at Blackpool. As we rushed down the side of a wave, it seemed as if we must plunge to the very bottom of the ocean. When we looked up we were surrounded by huge, green mountains of water which towered above us. Many, many times we closed our eyes and prayed, waiting for those mountains to collapse on top of us. As I looked up I thought, what if one of the sharks was up there, and fell down among us. Our minds were becoming confused.

The storm continued all day, whipping the spray over us and soaking us, so that our clothes clung to our bodies. The salt burned into our sun-blistered skin. Then, at about 8 pm, as suddenly as it had started, the wind and the sea died down. That night was the coldest of all, for with our wet clothes there was just no way of getting warm. The chief steward and I huddled together with our arms around each other.

"How would some of that stew do now, Jock?" he suddenly said to me, referring to the stew I had made such a fuss about on board the ship.

As the morning of the tenth day arrived, the heat of the rising sun began to thaw out our shivering, frozen bodies. But it would not be long until we cursed that sun. At night we prayed for the day to come, but when it did come, with its scorching hell, we prayed for the night, with its freezing cold. As I looked round the boat that day I was shocked by the deterioration of my mates during the night. The chief engineer, the chief steward and some of the Africans looked as if they could not stand up to much more. The storm and the cold of the previous night had sapped what little stamina we had left.

That night I huddled between the chief steward and the chief engineer. The latter told me that he still had a few years left before he was due to retire, but that if he survived this ordeal he would do so immediately. He had been at sea all his life but he had always wanted to open a chicken farm up in Perthshire.

The eleventh morning dawned and I was roused from an uneasy sleep to find that something was crushing my legs. I looked down and there, lying across my legs, was one of the African firemen. Thinking he was asleep, I bent over to waken him, for my legs were numb with his weight. When I looked closer I realised that for him, the journey was over. No longer would he have to endure the tortures of heat, cold and thirst, for he was dead. It may sound strange, but many of us envied him.

The Captain gave instructions in preparation for the burial. As he was African, it was left to the other Africans to carry out any traditions before he was cast over the aide. He was lifted and lay straddled across his mates' knees. They started a sort of wailing chant over his body. When they had finished, the Captain ordered the body to be propped on the side of the boat. It was to be held there until he read the burial service. When he arrived at the words, 'I commit this body to the deep,' the body was to be gently pushed over the side.

The Captain had almost arrived at the final words when somebody noticed that the body still wore a lifejacket, so he was pulled back aboard again and the struggle began to get the jacket off. It was quite a fight, for he had died with one arm folded across his chest. His other arm was stretched above his head and he was as stiff as a board. At last the jacket was removed and again he was propped on the side, held there by his African mates. The Captain again stumbled through the service. He did not have his glasses and the print on the little Testament had been blotted with dampness. I believe he said the service more from memory than from what he read. At last the final words were uttered, there was a splash and the body disappeared below the surface. Seconds later an arm broke surface and drifted astern, like a token of farewell. We followed that arm for the length of the boat, but as it slipped astern we turned our eyes away, for we knew those huge fins were right behind us. We did not want to know or to see, for any one of us might be next.

The death of the African lowered the morale in the boat. The chief steward was now only semi-conscious, and the chief engineer was looking very bad. As I sat there that day, I wondered who would be balanced on the side of the boat next.

The Captain, by his reckoning, thought that we should sight the Cape Verde islands late on the thirteenth day. He told us that there was a lighthouse and at night we were to keep a lookout for it. The first man to spot it would be given a large ration of water. He also said that there was an installation on one of the islands. According to the wireless operator there was very little life left in our transmitter batteries, but we might still pick up an oscillating sound from the station.

So, on the twelfth day we picked up our small transmitter, held it up and moved it slowly from right to left. We thought we could hear a slight sound, but it was so slight that we could not be sure. It could be imagination. The Captain however took a bearing on the compass, and we steered accordingly.

The thirteenth day arrived. By now, the chief steward was delirious and the chief engineer had taken a stroke. His mouth lay open and twisted and he was paralysed. Since the death of their mate the Africans had kept up their terrible, wailing chant. It was not the dreadful heat of day which bothered them, but the freezing cold of night. The rest of us were bothered by both. All that long day our bloodshot eyes searched the wilderness of sea ahead for a glimpse of the Promised Land, but anything we saw was in our minds and not in reality and the day passed like all the rest.

On the fourteenth day we tried out the transmitter again, but there was no response. Had the Captain made a mistake? Had we passed the islands? Were we all doomed to die? I looked across the gigantic, limitless ocean which curved away to infinity, glittering and sparkling beneath the blinding, incandescent sun, and I wondered how long it would take us to die.

The effects of exposure, fear and, above all, thirst were taking a heavy toll on us. Our minds were now becoming very confused indeed. Every now and again someone shouted, "Captain, Captain, there is a ship bearing down on us!" or, at night, "Light ahead!" Everyone's heart gave a great leap of joy, only to find it was a cruel trick by a hopeful

Group school photograph at Cornaigmore. Alex on second row, second from right

*Alex collecting water from the pump with his friend
Catriona and his dog*

A smart young Alex dressed up for his photo shoot

Catherine, Alex's mother, at the water pump.
There was no running water in the house

*Looking smart in his merchant seaman's uniform
which he was so proud to wear*

*Alex and Kenny who sailed together during the war
and later became brothers-in-law*

A portrait of Ella taken in April 1944

The marriage of Ella and Alex in February 1946.
The couple were devoted to each other

Alex with his children, Jean, Ronald and Alexandra.
A very proud dad

Probably the last family holiday together, at Prestwick

*Alex in his fifties. He was diagnosed with Alzheimer's
at the age of sixty*

Alex's favourite rock on the beautiful island of Tiree

imagination. Men cried bitterly from the crushing disappointment which followed. Some muttered to themselves. One man imagined he was out at his local with his wife.

"A brown ale for the missus, Jack, and the usual mild and bitter for me." He then picked up the imaginary pint before him and started to drink it, stopping to wipe the froth from his lips. Every man in that boat swallowed that pint, just as if it was right there.

So the fourteenth night began to settle in upon us. The sea was as smooth as I had ever seen it. The boat was cleaving through the still water, leaving a ghostly, gleaming trail of phosphorescence. The reddish glow of the sky was reflected on the sea, making it look as if we were sailing along on a sheet of copper. Tropical stars glittered. The full moon rose as if from the sea itself, and on we sailed.

The fifteenth day was now upon us. We searched the sky for a sign of rain, but there was nothing but that ball of fiery hell blazing mercilessly, torturing and mocking us.

Some men tried to squeeze out their urine to drink, but there was none. I thought of the big, juicy rats we had been in such a hurry to get rid of. We thought could see great ships all around us, but they were only great fins. We cursed our Navy and Air Force. Where the hell were they all? Were they all bloody blind?

Our hair and beards were all pure white with dried salt. Our faces had swollen, the skin hanging off where the salt had been baked by the scorching sun. Our tongues were beginning to swell, making our mouths hang open. Our eyes had sunk back in our swollen faces and they all had the same mad stare. Our backsides were raw with salt water boils and sores. Our feet had swollen to twice their normal size. All we wanted was to be as rich as the poorest hobo on land, for he had water.

That night I sat looking over the silver mirror of sea, the full moon sparkling and dancing on its surface. It was an awe inspiring scene. We seemed to be suspended in space on the very edge of the world. I looked over the side into the clear water, down through layer upon layer of depth. It seemed to me that the whole world had been a dream. It had died a thousand years before and all that was left of that dream was us and this small boat sailing forever across this endless ocean.

It was no longer the fear of dying that I felt, but the terrible fear of living; to go on and on, day following night, night following day. My tortured brain thought, why not jump over the side and sink into that beautiful depth, then drink and drink until my lungs and stomach burst? I looked over the side again and there, not five feet away, was a huge fin, keeping time with the boat.

As I sat there studying it, it reminded me of the children's sailing yachts I had seen on the ponds in Glasgow on a Sunday afternoon, away back in that dream of so long ago. When I looked again the fin had fallen behind out of sight. Again I thought of that beautiful depth of water drawing me like a magnet, and then, cutting across my thoughts, was my mother's voice, "There is no shame in fear, only in giving in to it. Someday people will look to you for comfort." The voice was so real that it seemed she had actually spoken in my ear. I had to put it down to the state of my mind.

I looked at the Captain with his uniform in rags, his gold braid hanging limply from his sleeves. There was the man my mother hoped I would become, but I knew then it could never be. His type of courage and endurance were qualities that few men possess. My mind drifted back to my mother and my beautiful island, which I would never see again. I thought of that last day my mother and I had spent on top of my favourite rock. Was it a thousand or a million years ago? What was it she had wanted to tell me? It must have been about my father. What kind of man had he been? Surely he must have been a very good man to marry a woman like my mother? Oh hell, I thought, what does it matter now?

I huddled down beside the chief steward and cradled his head in my arm and tried to comfort him. He kept calling for his wife. I brushed his fevered brow with water from the bottom of the boat and, in doing this, I too seemed to feel better. I was the youngest in the boat and because of that I would survive, of this I had suddenly become convinced.

"Damn it, Jock," a voice croaked beside me, "I wish to bloody hell I had stuck to trawlers. At least I could always get a mug of tea when

I wanted one." This man, like the Captain, was indestructible. Yes, I thought again, with men like these we must survive.

It was now 4 am on the sixteenth day. Another day of hell lay before us.

"Captain, Captain, I can see a light off the port bow," a voice croaked suddenly. Nobody bothered as we had heard it all before and we just could not face another disappointment. A few minutes passed and again the voice spoke, "Oh please, Captain, believe me." We all looked at the Captain's face. He was gazing steadily ahead, and then he spoke.

"Look ahead, men, and tell me what you see."

We looked ahead and there was nothing. There was a light and then there was nothing. Yes, there it was again. Was this just another cruel trick of the sea? We stared ahead for a few more minutes.

"There is a light, Captain. Oh God, there is a light," came a chorus of croaking voices.

"Men, we are saved. That is the light we have all been looking for, for it is a beacon which flashes every four seconds." said the Captain, his voice broken and full of emotion. "Men, let us now give thanks to God." He led us in prayer. Never have I known men pray with more feeling.

"Oh thank you, God, for being my pilot, in plotting a true course and delivering us from the perils of the deep," said the Captain, his voice rising above the rest, I looked across at him and thought how much we all owed that brilliant and brave man. I looked behind him and the fins had gone. For the first time I noticed that the boat was almost dry. We had had to give up pumping the previous day, for there was no one left with enough strength to do it.

As we sailed into the lee of the land our sail flapped uselessly against the mast, and though we were now in full view of the island[5], we could not muster enough strength among us to handle the heavy oars. We did not mind waiting for we knew we were safe. We had

---

5   São Vicente, in the north-west of the Cape Verde archipelago, located between the islands of Santo Antão and Santa Luzia. The island has a surface area of approximately 88 square miles.

distress rockets but they were useless, for they were soaking wet. Very slowly we drifted into the bay.

"Let's have a party, lads," the Captain said, "I think we all deserve it." The rest of the water was given out. The cook, being the man who first sighted the light, was given most of it. Working it out, it came to about three days' rations per man. Feeling that water going down my throat was something that could never be described in mere words.

It was now almost midday and still no-one had sighted us, but from the shore they would only see the top of our sail and they might take us for a fishing boat. It was only when we rose with the swell that we could see the shore clearly. We were not in the least concerned for all the time we were drifting in.

I glanced at the chief engineer who lay with his eyes shut and his mouth twisted open, and thought, never mind, old fellow, you will soon be all right. I looked at the chief steward. When we had spotted the light I had said to him, "Come on now, chief, you will soon be with your wife. We have sighted the light." He had mumbled something about there being no bloody light and that we were all doomed to die, but that he was alright now and would soon be home with his family. Then I thought about myself. What would I do? I would get another ship and go back to sea of course. It was the only life I knew and the only home I had.

I looked at the rest of those pathetic human beings and I felt so proud to be one of them. They had been to the very gates of hell. They had gone past the limits of human endurance and yet not one man had cracked. Not one man had given in to the terrible temptation of drinking seawater. The mutterings, the curses, the confusion of minds, the fears and the tears were not weaknesses. They were only part of being human.

I had learned things in that boat which I knew I would carry with me all my life. Now I knew what my mother had meant that day. We had known fear in that lifeboat such as I hoped I would never know again.

As we gazed again towards the shore we could see a lot of activity taking place. We had been sighted. Soon we were surrounded by an armada of small boats. As they pulled alongside us they threw lighted cigarettes into the boat among us. A man leaned over from one of the boats, tied a rope to our bow and started to tow us towards the shore. We were well and truly saved. The Captain had decided to take the tiller for those last few hundred yards. I saw him slump unconscious across the tiller, but his hand was still clasped around it. The natives in the boats kept looking at us as if we were from Mars, and who could blame them? We must have looked a frightening and weird lot. A lighted cigarette landed on my knee. I grabbed it, inhaled deeply, and passed out.

Chapter Seven

Rescue

When I regained consciousness I found myself lying on a mattress on the floor of what turned out to be a sort of hotel. I looked around and found most of my mates lying beside me. The officers had been taken to a large room upstairs and the chief engineer and the chief steward had been taken to the tiny hospital. The Africans had been taken to another place among the natives of the island, who were also black, being Portuguese West Africans. The building was by no stretch of the imagination what we would call a hotel, being more like a huge hut, but to us it was better than any five star hotel at home.

The black doctor on the island moved among us as we lay about the floor. I was surprised to find that he could speak very good English but it transpired that he had spent his student days in London. A native girl, probably a nurse, was assisting the doctor. She held a mirror in her hands and she let everyone have a look at himself. When my turn came and I looked into that mirror, I got the shock of my life. My black hair, of which I had plenty, was pure white with salt, and so was my beard. My shirt hung in rags and was also caked with salt. Layers of burned skin hung from my face, which was badly swollen. My eyes seemed to have sunk right to the back of my head, and they had a mad and haunted stare about them. My feet had swollen to twice their normal size. From my feet to my thighs I had a mass of sores and boils caused by the salt water. As I looked in that mirror I felt horrified. Surely this was not me? Was I to remain a Frankenstein for the rest of my life? I had seen my mates change, but it had not occurred to me that I was also changing.

The doctor came over to examine me. He told me that I was in a surprisingly good condition. I asked him about my appearance and with a laugh he assured me that after a good wash and shave I would look and feel a lot better. The swelling would subside in a few days.

"The scars on your body I can heal. The scar on your mind is something only time can heal," he said.

Native women came in then and gently removed our tattered clothing. We were bathed down where we lay. Two native men came in and shaved us, which was a rather painful operation. The salt was washed from our hair and we could actually smell the fresh water, but the doctor had forbidden us to drink any. Next, our sores were covered over with soothing ointment and bandaged. We were dressed in white short sleeved shirts and white shorts. Again the mirror was passed around and I was surprised by the difference in my appearance. We were then given small quantities of fruit juice.

When we were in the boat we had dreamed of little else but the gallons upon gallons of water we would consume if we survived, and yet here we were sipping fruit juice. The doctor explained to us that we would have to get our stomachs accustomed slowly to food and liquids, otherwise we would suffer terribly from cramp. Now that we knew we could get water however, we were no longer thirsty. The doctor told us he would give us a sedative, and after a good night's sleep we would feel much stronger. After taking the sedative we all fell into the glorious dark valley of sleep, the first real sleep we had had in all those long, long nights.

The following morning I awoke to find Jack looking down at me, saying, "Come on, Jock. You have been sleeping for almost fourteen hours. Don't you think it is time you were up and about? I will help you to your feet." As I stood up the floor seemed to swing at a crazy angle. Jack and I, holding on to each other, started to stagger about. We were like babies taking their first steps. The floor rose and fell below us, but as we continued we began to get steadier. Then we started to get everybody else on their feet, and assisting them to walk. It took us a few days to rid ourselves of the restless motion of the boat.

After breakfast the British Consul came in and gave us good news. Our mates in the other lifeboat were safe. They had been picked up, after spending ten days in their boat, by a British corvette. They had told the commanding officer about us, but he had explained that he must pick up a convoy in Freetown and that owing to heavy seas, he was already behind schedule, so he could only spend a very limited time looking for us. As a result he did what could only be done in the direst of emergencies; he broke his wireless seal and sent a message to Gibraltar, giving a rough calculation of the area where we might be found. We were told how a naval vessel and a Sunderland flying boat had been despatched to search the area. All northbound ships had been advised to keep a sharp lookout for us. The island we were now on had been informed we were heading for it and the natives had lit a huge bonfire every night on the highest point in the hope that we would see it. We had sailed on, unaware of all that was being done to find us. I regretted the curses I had poured on our Navy and Air Force. After all, we had been only a very small speck on a very huge ocean.

The news that our mates were safe was like a tonic to us. During that storm we had wondered how they were faring. I had wondered too which of us would arrive first at the islands, or whether both boats were to perish in those raging seas. Now I knew we were all safe.

Shortly after the Consul left the Captain came down and told us that the chief steward and the chief engineer had both died within fifteen minutes of each other. We received this news with a feeling of great loss and shock. It seemed so cruel that we had survived so much together and now they were gone. It was a terrible blow.

The following day we prepared ourselves to attend the double funeral. We were a sorry looking lot. We had been given large white tropical helmets and we all wore white tropical shorts and white sandals several sizes too big, to allow for our still swollen feet. From our shorts down to our sandals our legs were bound in white bandages. Most of us were limping badly and we were still holding on to each other for support, but we would still have attended those funerals if it had meant crawling on our hands and knees. There were a few cars and those who could barely walk were taken by car.

As we stood outside the small white hospital, it seemed as if every native on the island had turned out. Everyone seemed to carry bunches of flowers. We were given many bunches by the natives and flowers were thrown at us in gestures of kindness and respect. We were surprised to see two rows of Portuguese naval sailors standing to attention on either side of the main door of the hospital. The first coffin emerged, quickly followed by the second, both borne by Portuguese naval officers. Slowly they passed through the two lines of white clad sailors, then turned and headed for the little cemetery which lay three hundred yards up a narrow, winding road. The cemetery was reserved for white people only, for example missionaries or such people.

When we entered the cemetery the natives were not allowed to enter, but I believe the reason was that there was not enough room for everyone inside. Gently, the coffins were laid on boards which lay across the graves, which were side by side. The officers took the cords and our mates were laid to rest. The Consul started to read the service and as he read, the natives, who had been making an awful noise, became silent. A hush seemed to fall over the island, disturbed only by the swell of the sea as it broke on the nearby shore and the drone of the Consul's voice. I looked down to where the chief engineer lay and I wondered if he had died happy, dreaming of his chicken farm in the green, rolling hills of Perthshire, so far away. I looked at where the chief steward lay and his words came floating back to me, "How would some of that stew do now, Jock?" Hot tears rolled down my swollen cheeks, burning them like acid.

Standing there in our weak condition with the sun beating down on us was in itself quite an ordeal, but to add to our distress we had been given large doses of laxatives by the doctor. I was feeling great discomfort from the effects of this and was doing my best to control the situation. As the Consul came to the words, 'dust to dust,' there was suddenly the crash of a heavy gun nearby. This happened so unexpectedly and our nerves being as they were, most of us lost control and found ourselves in a very embarrassing position. We did not know that a Portuguese man of war had been lying at anchor out in the bay, hence all the sailors. At a prearranged signal she had fired her heavy gun in salute to our dead.

The island itself must have made Devil's Island look like paradise, by comparison. It had not rained there for a year and much to our amusement, we discovered that water was rationed[6]. It had to be shipped across from another island about ten miles away. However there was more than enough for our needs. We were allowed to have a bath every day, but two or three used the same water. The bath consisted of a barrel cut in half, in which we stood while an elderly native woman sponged us down. At first we felt rather embarrassed, but it seemed to be the custom. Nothing appeared to grow anywhere on the island; the earth was just brown clay baked hard by the blazing sun. The flowers for the funerals must have been brought in with the water. I often thought of my own island with its various shades of green and all the different colours which come from the millions of daisies, buttercups and other flowers which grow there. But to us, this island was paradise. It was solid and safe.

We were treated like heroes by all and had complete freedom to go anywhere we wanted. We were warned about swimming in the sea as sharks came very close to the beach. Some of the natives had only one leg to prove it. We did not have to be told however, as we already knew the danger only too well.

As we waited for our departure, a rumour spread about that a German U-boat was lying off the island, waiting to intercept the Portuguese ship which would take us to Lisbon and that some of us would be taken as prisoners back to Germany. At first we laughed at such a ridiculous idea, but later we began to wonder if such a thing could be possible. The more we thought about it, the more we became convinced that it could and probably would happen, for although Portugal was a neutral country, that did not make much difference in those days.

We had now been on the island for a week and were told that we would leave at the end of the second week. The night before our departure I took a walk down to where our lifeboat had been dragged

---

6   The island of São Vicente has no permanent natural water source and is extremely arid, with an average annual rainfall of 80 to 130 mm.

up on to the beach. When I approached it, I was surprised to find the boat under guard by two Portuguese sailors. It seemed the natives had been taking bits away as souvenirs and since the boat had to be shipped back home, it must be guarded. As I came nearer I expected the guards to turn me away, but to my surprise they came to attention and saluted me as I passed. I felt very proud and honoured; for it was not me that they were showing their admiration for, but our Merchant and Royal Navies.

As I stood beside that frail boat, it seemed unbelievable that it had carried twenty-eight of us those hundreds of miles across the South Atlantic. I looked at the planks that had been below the sea. It was nothing short of a miracle that the boat had survived that storm. As I remembered all our positions I pictured the chief engineer and the chief steward as they had lain in the boat. Looking out over the smooth sea I thought about how they had given their whole lives to that sea, and now it had taken those lives from them. I glanced up the hill to the little cemetery where they lay side by side. For them at least, the war was finished, and they were at peace with the troubled world.

That night the British Consul threw a farewell party in our honour and all the white people attended. We were wined and dined and had we been royalty, we could not have been treated with more respect. Everybody wanted to hear about our adventures at sea. We all had a wonderful time that night.

Anchored in the bay the next morning was the ship that would take us on our six day voyage to Lisbon. She was quite a large cargo passenger ship of about five thousand tons, but what drew our attention was her glistening white paintwork. We had become so used to seeing our ships painted overall with sombre Admiralty grey that it was strange to see a ship painted in peacetime colours. In large golden letters along her sides was the word 'Portugal', so that the U-boats would know that she was neutral.

As we headed down towards the water tender that was to take us out to the ship, it seemed that the whole island had turned out to see us off. The native women flung their arms around us and smothered us with kisses. The men chanted some kind of song, but we did not know what it meant. It was all very wonderful.

We stepped on board the ship and the Captain and all the officers lined up to welcome us on board. As we passed each officer, we shook hands with him. Using an interpreter, the Captain told us how proud he was to have British merchant seamen on board his ship, and how proud Portugal was of the great battle we were fighting in the Atlantic. He said that he had given orders that we were to be given the complete freedom of the ship and we could even go up on the bridge any time we wished. This is a very great privilege on any passenger ship, extended to only the most important passengers.

The rest of the passengers had already heard about us and they had all insisted that it would be a great honour if they could have some of us at each of their tables. We were taken aback by the royal treatment which we were receiving, but we were also enjoying it immensely.

The table I was asked to join was occupied by two wealthy looking business men and their wives. It was quite amusing as we could not speak to each other. We sat nodding and smiling at each other throughout the meal. If I wanted something passed to me from the table I pointed and signalled and they nodded and smiled. When at last they realised I was asking for something, they passed up everything except the one item I required.

On the second day out, as I was sitting at the table, there was a terrific roar. I almost jumped over the table with fright. I could have sworn it was the roar of a lion, but I knew that was stupid. One does not find lions out at sea. I looked at my companions but they seemed quite unconcerned, and gave me their usual nod and smile. After the meal I decided to find out where the noise had come from. I met Jack and as he also had heard it, we went together down to the 'tween deck, where the cargo was stored. There, to our amazement, was a huge cage which held a ferocious looking lion. Not only that, we also had apes and monkeys. The ship had been to the coast of Africa and was bringing them back to the zoo in Lisbon. I was glad we were on a neutral ship with little chance of being sunk, for I did not relish the idea of sharing a lifeboat with a full grown African lion. I had an idea the lion would not be the one to go hungry.

I shared a cabin with two Portuguese gentlemen and I found it difficult to sleep, as they both snored very loudly. I was lying in the dark one night, when suddenly I heard the ship's telegraph ringing and the engines slowing down. I heard running feet on the deck above me. I leapt from my bunk and, as I raced for the upper deck, I thought, 'This German U-boat has stopped the ship to take us prisoner. There can be no other explanation for the ship stopping in mid-Atlantic.' It was perhaps selfish of me, but when I arrived on deck I felt relieved to discover that one of the Portuguese soldiers had either jumped or fallen overboard. The ship turned about and in sweeping circles searched the area for the unfortunate soldier, but in vain. I thought again of those huge fins, and shuddered.

The day before we were due to arrive in Lisbon our Captain asked us all to join him in the ship's dining room. He warned us that when we docked we would most likely be interviewed by many reporters. He told us we were not to answer any questions, but to refer everyone to him, the reason being that Lisbon was full of German agents, so the less we said the better[7]. Sure enough, as soon as we tied up in Lisbon the following day, we were swamped by reporters of all nationalities, who took photographs and wanted to know all about our experiences in the open boat. We did as we had been told however and referred them to our Captain. The next day we had a big write-up in the Portuguese

---

7 Portugal was officially neutral during the Second World War, however the Estado Novo, led by António de Oliveira Salazar, maintained a delicate political balance, exporting materials to the Allies, the Axis Powers and other neutral countries throughout. Its capital, Lisbon, as the only remaining free port in Europe, was flooded with refugees seeking passage to the US or South America and consequently was home to numerous intelligence agents of different nationalities, including the legendary 'Garbo', as well as to writers such as Ian Fleming. This period has been extensively written about, both in fiction and non-fiction; see for example *Double Cross* by Ben MacIntyre and *A Small Death in Lisbon* by Robert Wilson.

newspapers, but as we could not read Portuguese, we did not know what was being said about us.

After all the formalities had been dealt with we were taken to our hotel, a huge building not far from the docks which had been converted into large dormitories. Inside were two hundred British merchant seamen survivors like ourselves. We later discovered that there were over four hundred merchant seamen survivors in Lisbon at that time, all waiting to be shipped home to Britain. Every one of those men had been torpedoed. One crew had been in their lifeboat for twenty days. We knew only too well how those men had suffered but like us, all they wanted was to get home, spend their month's survivor's leave with their families and then return to the battle to face, perhaps, another twenty days in a lifeboat. I thought to myself, 'how can we lose this battle when there are so many bloody idiots like us, who, because the challenge of the sea is in our blood, and because we know no other way of life, will keep going back, knowing full well that we will die.' Some would be burned alive in a sea of burning oil. Others would sail across an endless ocean, dying of thirst, sailing on and on until their tongues swelled and choked them, or they went mad and jumped over the side, among those deadly fins, just to show them that they too, could swim. Perhaps, if they were fortunate, they would be drawn with their ship down into those unknown depths and death would come mercifully fast. The sea, to those who understood it as we did, was like a man's spirit singing to his heart, probably the last sound that many of us would ever hear.

Chapter Eight

City of Spies

We were destined to stay in Lisbon for almost a month. It was one of the most beautiful cities I had visited during my travels, and one of the most exciting. The city was full of intrigue. There were many German intelligence agents based there, so we had been well warned to be on our guard and to be very careful about the company we kept.

What struck me most about the city was the complete absence of any signs of war. At night the place was ablaze with lights and neon signs. The shops were packed with all the good things that British shops had not seen since the conflict began. From here the war felt many thousands of miles distant and yet the grim battle of the Atlantic was being waged in all its terrible ferocity not more than five miles away, with British ships and seamen being blown to bits. Only three miles distant German U-boats were lying in wait for their victims.

The day after we arrived in Lisbon we were taken to the British Consul's office, where we were told that everything possible was being done to find transport to take us home, but as there were so many of us it would take some time. In the meantime we would be given ten shillings a week as pocket money, to buy cigarettes. The rest of our expenses were paid by the British Government.

The street on which the Consul's offices were situated was on a slight incline and as we looked up the street, we could see the Union Jack, the Stars and Stripes and the Swastika all hanging more or less side-by-side. Oh yes, Lisbon was indeed a city of intrigue and many surprises, but as it was a neutral country the Germans had as much right to be there as we had.

After leaving the Consul we were taken to a tailor, who must have been blessing the war for the amount of trade it had brought him. There we were fitted with suits. The material was of poor quality, with very jazzy stripes, and was certainly not what most of us would have chosen. Still, we could hardly arrive back home in Britain wearing tropical shorts and sun helmets.

Jack and I were constant companions; the relationship between us being like that of father and son. We seemed to have so much in common. He had never been married and like me, he had no home. We were both just fellow travellers on the oceans of the world. In the evenings we perused the numerous dockside fish-bars. These places sold every conceivable kind of shellfish, including lobster, crab and octopus. They also sold cheap Portuguese beer made from onions, which, though not very palatable was quite potent and was the best we could afford with our few shillings.

One night, Jack and I were sitting in one of these bars, discussing how nice it would be to have enough money to buy a decent British meal of steak, washed down by a good old cup of tea. In Lisbon tea was more expensive than Scotch whisky. Although the food at the hotel was quite good, it always consisted of some type of fish, washed down by a horrible tasting table wine. As we sat there, two men at another table kept looking over at us. They were rather well dressed for a dockside fish-bar. I watched them for a while and sensed, as they kept glancing over, that they were talking about us. After a while, I drew Jack's attention to them.

"They are Germans, Jock. Don't you know one by looking at him?"

"No," I replied, "how can you tell?"

"By the shape at the back of their heads, Jock. Their heads are straight at the back while ours have a curve where it comes down to join the neck."

"How do you know all this, Jack?"

"Well Jock, in the years I spent on trawlers before the war I met many Germans. I found them quite a decent lot in those days."

"Excuse me, gentlemen," interrupted one of the men. "My friend and I have been laying bets with each other. I say you are English and he says you are Portuguese."

"Well, you are not entirely right," I replied. "You see, my friend here is English but I come from Scotland."

"Well, well, this is wonderful! We both come from England but we have not been home to Britain since the war started. Would you mind if we joined you? I am sure we have many things to talk about."

"Certainly," replied Jack. "Why not, indeed?"

The German then turned and walked back to his companion, and as he did so, Jack whispered urgently to me, "Listen, Jock, don't be fooled. They are Germans alright. Leave this to me. I'll do the talking." I thought to myself, 'They are not Germans. Their English is perfect, without even a trace of an accent.' Yet I knew that Jack was a wily old fox. The men drew their chairs up to our table and asked what we would like to drink. They told us they were both civil airline pilots and they certainly would have passed as such, both being very well dressed. They were tall, well-built, good looking men and it became obvious to us that they were also well educated.

Again they stated that they had not been in England since the war began. This in itself seemed rather strange to us. Their jobs would surely have brought them home at some point. We also wondered why they were not flying with the RAF, for they were both young men. However, we did not voice these questions. Their knowledge of England was actually a lot better than ours and had it not been for the shape of their heads and the little things that did not seem to add up, we could quite easily have believed them. However we were too suspicious to be taken in.

It must have been obvious to them that we were Merchant seamen, since there were about four hundred other survivors walking about Lisbon wearing almost the same suit. To my amazement, Jack proceeded to tell them a story that sounded so true that even I almost began to believe him. He said that we had had to leave the convoy with engine trouble and had limped into Lisbon to carry out repairs. Because he knew that they would be well informed about all that was going on at the docks, he told them that we had just arrived a couple of hours before. He said that we had taken advantage of the fact that one did not require clothing coupons in Lisbon, and had got a sub from the Captain to buy the suits we were now wearing. We had gone back to the ship to get dressed and after being told by the engineers that we would not be leaving until the following day, we had decided to come ashore to spend what little money we had left, which was not much after buying the suits. Our two companions seemed very impressed. They told us not to worry about money as they had sufficient, and asked us to accompany them to a better place for a meal. We protested, of course, but they insisted and so we played along.

We eventually arrived at a very expensive looking restaurant, where we were handed menus. Jack and I chose nice big, thick steaks. I remember looking at that steak lying on my plate and thinking that it must be worth about three weeks' rations of meat at home. By this time I was beginning to feel rather apprehensive about the whole affair, but Jack seemed to have the situation well in hand. After our steaks we ordered tea instead of coffee. I think it was the most wonderful tea we had ever tasted. Our hosts ordered drinks and then started to ply us with questions. How was good old Blighty standing up to those terrible air raids? Jack replied that although there were indeed many raids, the damage inflicted was slight compared to the losses the German Air Force was suffering. They asked us about the war at sea. Again we told them that we did not think Germany could keep this battle going much longer, as the number of U-boats being lost was considerable. We said that we had recently sailed in a convoy in which we had seen no less than four U-boats destroyed, without the loss of a single ship.

After we had had our meal and before the drink had taken too much effect, we decided it was time to make our exit. We excused ourselves to go to the toilet. As Jack and I rose and made our way out of the dining room we saw a door, which on opening led out on to a side street, much to our relief. We laughed as we ran down the narrow, cobbled back streets of Lisbon. If they were German agents, what a surprise they would get when they checked the docks for a ship which did not exist. They owed us those steaks for the hungry days we had suffered. But what if they were not Germans at all? Well, in that case we had played a dirty trick on two very nice guys, but we were certainly not going back to make sure. Anyway, Jack had no doubts in his mind.

At the beginning of our second week in Lisbon the Captain came to wish us all a safe voyage home. He shook hands with each one of us in turn and thanked us for the part we had played in those sixteen long days. He would never forget us, he said. We did not have to tell him that we would never forget him, not as long as any of us lived. He said that he did not want to leave us, but he and the rest of the officers were being flown home and even a Captain had to obey orders.

The day after the Captain's departure the British Consul came to our hotel and addressed us, looking very worried. That morning, it seemed, Germany had told Portugal that she was harbouring too many British seamen and that if she wanted to remain neutral, she had until the end of the week to get us out. We were told that married men would be given priority. The authorities would fly as many as possible out and the remainder would go by sea.

Portugal had conveniently decided to sell Britain two small trawlers which were berthed in Lisbon. The survivors could sail them to Gibraltar, where they would probably be converted into minesweepers, but the minute they sailed out of the three mile neutral zone they were liable to be sunk. As the ships had no armaments or protection against mines it was a very dangerous mission.

The following night the first trawler left, filled with survivors. It seemed as if the whole of Lisbon knew she was leaving, so it was pretty obvious the Germans knew as well. The next day Jack and I went to the Merchant Navy Club for a game of billiards and there we heard the sad news that the trawler had sunk with heavy casualties. Some said she had been shelled by a U-boat while others said she had struck a mine. We never found out what happened, but she had certainly sunk. On board were the crew that had survived twenty days in the lifeboats. The survivors had been picked up by a naval vessel so at least they had a chance of reaching home.

The next day the second trawler sailed in broad daylight, which seemed the height of madness to us. Every agent in Lisbon would know, and in turn every German plane and U-boat in the area. This time many of our crew were among those on board. It was an emotional moment as we all shook hands when they left the hotel to go on board the trawler. We had all been through so much together. The knowledge that the other ship had been sunk did not ease the situation. How we prayed that they would arrive in Gibraltar safely.

Now there were only sixty-five of us left in Lisbon. The end of the week was almost upon us, and the deadline Germany had given Portugal. Jack and I speculated about what would happen if they did not get us out in time. Maybe Portugal would be forced to hold us prisoner until the end of the war? On the other hand, Germany might demand that we should be handed over to them. We felt like rats caught in a trap. We could stay where we were to be interned, be handed over to Germany as prisoners of war, or we could sail out, perhaps to be blown to bits. The situation was full of suspense.

Jack and I were probably the least concerned among the lot of us about the position. If we were held by Portugal we would be well treated and while we did not relish the thought of being handed over to Germany, we at least knew that we had no relatives worrying about us. With regard to the alternative of being blown to bits, we had always intended to go back to sea and this was just a risk that every seaman had to face.

It was now Friday evening and the deadline would probably expire at midnight. As the hours ticked by, with still no word of what was to happen to us, the tension grew. We were like prisoners already as we were confined to the hotel with strict instructions not to leave under any pretext, in case some word came through. By 10 pm it looked as if the war at sea would have to get on without us. Then we heard a lot of voices downstairs and footsteps approaching our dormitory. Some decision had been made. What was it?

The door opened and in walked the British Consul, accompanied by another two men. He told us that we must be ready to leave within five minutes. The two men who were with him would act as guides to take us down to the docks, where we would embark on a small ship which would take us to Gibraltar. Then he gave us the wonderful news that the second trawler had arrived safely in Gibraltar and ended by wishing us a safe voyage. After the Consul left the guides split us into two parties. Each party would take a different route to the docks. We were instructed not to speak or to make any noise, as they did not want any attention drawn to our departure; an almost impossible task in Lisbon at that time.

We all walked stealthily through the back streets of Lisbon and I wondered if messages were already being sent to the U-boats. I thought that perhaps it would have been better if we had been interned. At least then we might still be alive at the end of the war. As I watched the dark shadows of my mates I wondered how many of us would live to see the end of it all. In fact, I wondered how many of us would still be alive to see the following dawn.

At last we arrived at the docks and led by our guide, we headed for a small coastal ship. She reminded me of the little colliers on which I had sailed up and down U-boat Alley. Her funnel and bridge were aft and her foredeck was taken up by one long hold. We were expected to go down into the hold where there were straw mattresses, better known to seamen as 'donkeys' breakfasts', which were probably crawling with lice. This meant that if the ship struck a mine, or was sinking for any other reason, we would be trapped like rats, with no chance of survival. For this reason we decided to put on the hatch covers and stay on deck. This also had disadvantages; we would have no protection from the elements and in the case of us being machine gunned from the air, we would have no cover. However, we decided that staying on top of the hatch was the lesser of two evils. At least we would be able to say our prayers before we died.

A check was made to see that all sixty-five of us were on board. This was confirmed, so silently we slipped our moorings and headed for the open sea. Would we be able to evade the U-boats which lay in wait outside the three mile limit? We would not have long to wait to find out.

As we gathered speed I cursed the ship's motor engines. With the noise they were making every U-boat for miles around must hear us coming. I felt some small consolation in the fact that this little ship had made the run to Gibraltar many times before, ferrying refugees from Lisbon. Rumour had it too that she was being used for another purpose. Apparently special cameras had been built into her navigation lights to enable her to take photographs of the Spanish coast, as Britain suspected that the Germans were using bases on this coast for their U-boats. This may have been a fairy tale but in those days anything was feasible, no matter how crazy it may have sounded.

The lights of Lisbon slowly disappeared and the darkness of the night settled around us. The ship began to rise and fall as we headed further and further into the long, slow swell of the open sea, leaving the safety of neutral waters behind. As we peered into the darkness ahead we could see the white tops of the waves as they rolled towards and then past us. I thought that at least we would get some warning of attack as it was obvious that no U-boat would waste a torpedo to sink a ship of this size. They would sink her with shellfire and so I kept a lookout for the warning flash which would tell us that a shell was arriving within seconds.

The ship swung into the full swell of the Atlantic, dipping her bow deeper into the oncoming sea. The waves broke over her, soaking us to the skin. I peered into the darkness ahead, my eyes smarting from the salt spray, and saw two dark shapes suddenly appear. Everyone held their breath. Were they U-boats? No, they couldn't be, they were too high in the water. To our great relief we realised they were two armed trawlers sent to escort us to Gibraltar. Though we were shivering with fear, dampness and cold we gave a cheer which made the 'Hampden Roar' sound like a whisper. They had been waiting to pick us up when we left the neutral zone.

Dawn started to break, giving the white topped sea a cold and forlorn appearance which matched our own. We were stiff and cramped in our wet clothes. I was beginning to wonder if we had not been more comfortable in the lifeboat when at last pint mugs of boiling tea, accompanied by huge corned beef sandwiches were passed around and I felt ashamed at even making the comparison.

There could never be anything to compare with those days, at least I hoped not.

I watched Jack scoff at least three mugs of tea and thought that as long as he had a smoke and a plentiful supply of tea he could face anything the war had to offer. I wondered why he had never married and settled down and as I studied him, I realised that he was old enough to be my father. Again I wondered what he had been like in his younger days. I wondered too if I, unlike Jack, would ever meet a girl with whom I could settle down, supposing I survived the war? I had had many girls in many ports but, like the typical sailor, I had loved them and left them, for I was really only in love with one thing – the sea. Perhaps someday, like a woman scorned, the sea would punish me. I looked again at Jack. Yes, he was in love, but like me, only with the sea.

The hot tea and the warmth of the sun put us in better spirits. The sight of those two faithful escorts, one on each side of us, with machine guns pointing in all directions, their gunners wrapped in their duffle coats keeping their lonely vigil beside them and now and again giving us a cheery wave, made us feel so safe that someone among us started to sing the hit tune of the day, 'Roll out the Barrel'. Within minutes we had all joined in. One chap produced a mouth organ which, he told us, he had stolen from a street barrow in Lisbon, when the vendor wasn't looking. Nevertheless I was quite sure he would arrive in heaven with no black marks against his name for the enjoyment he gave us. Then began another tune called 'Red Sails in the Sunset', sung no doubt for our benefit. It made us think again of the lifeboat, for they all had red sails. And so we went through all the wartime songs, our voices travelling over the sea so loudly that one of our escorts signalled that he had just received a message from a couple of U-boats asking would we mind if they came up and joined in the chorus. As we sang I thought what a bloody crazy nation we are.

Suddenly, above our singing we heard the dreaded wailing of action stations ringing out on our escorts. An unidentified aircraft was approaching. Our singing stopped and the blood froze in our veins. Again I could smell the now familiar odour of human fear. Perhaps doctors can explain this[8]? The only explanation I can give is that possibly the glands of the body become overactive and produce some kind of fluid which emits this odour, but there is no doubt in my mind that one can smell human fear. If this was an enemy aircraft we had good reason to be afraid, for we had no chance if he decided to machine-gun us, exposed as we were. To our great relief it turned out to be one of our own Catalina flying boats, probably sent out from Gibraltar to look for us. It circled the area and then, satisfied that there were no U-boats in the vicinity, swooped low over us in a farewell salute and disappeared.

Gradually, out of the haze ahead, we began to distinguish the great rock rising from the sea. We had made it. It had taken thirty-six hours from Lisbon and we were tired, hungry and cold. As we approached the entrance to Gibraltar harbour, our escorts altered their positions so that one was ahead of us, the other astern. We slowly steamed up the harbour between the lines of all the great battleships tied to their moorings: the *Rodney*, the *Nelson*, the *Malaya*, the aircraft carrier *Formidable*, the minelayers *Manxman* and *Welshman* as well as all the cruisers and destroyers. Thousands of sailors in white tropical uniform lined their rails and cheered us as we sailed past. Merchant ships gave us a hoot on their sirens. Not a single one of us on that small ship did not brush a tear from his eye, and for us all it was our finest hour.

I looked at those mighty ships with their still mightier guns and those thousands of youthful sailors and I knew then that we would win the battle of the seas. It might take a long time, but we would win. The ships of all nations would once again be as free as the sea on which they sailed. My only doubt was whether I would survive to see it all happen.

---

8   A study was carried out in 2008 by Dr Lilianne Mujica-Parodi, a cognitive neuroscientist at Stony Brook University in New York. See www.newscientist.com/article/dn17527-scent-of-fear-puts-brain-in-emergency-mode/

Chapter Nine

Operation Torch

Once tied up at the dockyard we were lined up on the quay-side and what a bedraggled bunch we looked. The cheap material of the suits which we had been given in Lisbon had shrunk with the soaking we had received, making them look quite ridiculous. However, they would probably have to do us until we arrived home.

A young British Army officer, accompanied by a sergeant, walked down the line and as they drew abreast of me, they stopped.

"Do you happen to have your identity card, old chap?" the officer asked.

"No," I replied, with a serious face, "but I can tell you where you will find it."

"Where would that be, old chap?" asked the officer.

"Somewhere in Davy Jones' Locker, three hundred miles west of the Canary Islands," I replied.

Seeing the young officer become rather embarrassed, I pulled out the document with which we had all been issued in Lisbon. It contained my photograph, fingerprints and the name of the ship on which I had been sailing when sunk.

"Perhaps this will save you a long search," I said, with a grin.

Eventually we were put into army lorries and taken to our hotel. After a hot bath and a good meal we began to feel like human beings again. To our delight, we met our mates who had been shipped out from Lisbon before us on the second trawler. They had joined up with a convoy heading for Gibraltar. Now we knew the reason they had left Lisbon in daylight. It had all been neatly arranged before they left.

As the days dragged on, Jack and I became more and more fed-up hanging about with no funds but our ten shillings pocket money. As each day passed, we expected news to come through that we were about to be shipped home. At the beginning of the second week we both decided to go down to the shipping office and sign on, if we could get places together on a ship. After all, what did it matter to us if we came back to the UK or not? We both had a month's survivor's leave to come, but we could take that anytime once we reached home. So off we went to see the shipping master and explained the situation to him.

"I think the two of you must be off your heads!" was his reaction. "However, as it so happens, we have a Royal Fleet Auxiliary tanker looking for an AB and a bosun, if you are really interested." He went on to explain that it was a two year station, but the men we were replacing had already done one year and eight months of the two year articles, leaving us with four months to do. This suited us very well as we were guaranteed a passage home at the end of the four months and we both signed on, Jack as bosun and I as AB. The shipping master's parting words to us were, "Now I know you are both bloody mad."

We returned to the hotel to tell our mates the good news. Our excitement changed to disgust when they told us the news which had just come through – that they were being taken home the following day, on no less a ship than the battleship *Malaya*. We both felt very disappointed but there was nothing we could do about it.

We wished our mates goodbye and safe journey home and headed for a place called the Cormorant Steps, where all the liberty boats from the ships lying out at anchor brought their crews ashore. We hitched a lift on one of the boats out to our new ship, which was lying in the centre of the harbour, tied up to buoys.

She was a fairly large tanker of some eight thousand tons. Our job for the next four months was to sail down the Mediterranean with the convoys to fuel the escort vessels, destroyers, corvettes and such like at sea. When we had used all our fuel we would leave the convoy and return to Gibraltar unescorted, to re-fuel ready for the next convoy.

Mostly we carried heavy crude oil, but we also carried aviation spirits, which were highly dangerous.

The following day Jack and I watched the tugs as they began to manoeuvre the *Malaya*, with all our mates on board, away from the quayside, better known to those familiar with Gibraltar as the Mole. The destroyers slipped their moorings and made their way out of the harbour in readiness to escort the battleship home. As the tugs drew her out into the centre of the harbour we could see our mates waving to us from the shadows of their huge guns. We watched as the great ship made for the entrance to the harbour and our mates became little specks in the distance. They were going home to their loved ones. They would have at least a month's survivor's leave and for some perhaps, an honourable discharge from the war. Jack and I felt very lonely and homesick for the homes that neither of us had. I thought that perhaps it would be nice to have someone to whom I could return. Brushing such sentiments from my mind, I thought that although I would have loved to have sailed in a battleship, for us it was time to return to the sea and the war.

The next day we put to sea. There was a large convoy lying out in the Gibraltar Straits and we watched the now familiar sight of the ships raising their anchors. The destroyers bustled here and there and then the long columns of ships assumed the shape of a convoy. We took up the rear of one of the columns to enable the destroyers to come up astern of us. We could then feed our pipeline across and pump our oil into them, just like a patient being given a blood transfusion. Indeed, our oil was just as vital to those destroyers as blood was to a patient. Slowly we headed down the Mediterranean, our destination Malta. A Maltese convoy was always regarded as second only to a Russian Convoy in terms of danger. All was quiet until we arrived at Bonn Point and then the dreaded alert sounded. Enemy aircraft were approaching.

I had been allocated a twin Marlene machine gun. As I began to strap myself in I could hear the distant roar of approaching aircraft. I swung the gun around in the direction of the sound and was appalled to see wave after wave of planes approaching low over the convoy.

Already the destroyers had opened fire and then the Merchant ships joined in the chorus. The first wave of dive bombers shrieked down on us like demons from hell, followed by a second, then a third wave. They seemed to fill the air like migrating birds. Ships began to blaze and sink to port and starboard and we had to keep zigzagging to avoid stricken ships ahead of us. One ship had her funnel and bridge blown clean off by an aerial torpedo. Planes exploded in the air as our bullets found their marks. One plane which had been hit was blazing like a torch and it came screaming towards us, out of control. I felt sure it must explode on our deck, but it skimmed over us and plunged into the sea. A great spout of water rose up in the air and when it subsided all that was left were a few pieces of wreckage floating on the surface. Still they came in, determined to wipe every last one of us off the surface of the sea. All our guns became red-hot and then, as suddenly as it had all started, it stopped and the planes wheeled away. We knew they would be back however and we were not proved wrong.

The following morning, as the grey dawn streaked the sky, back they came. This time I was at the helm. My mate on the watch was also a gunner and he had taken over the machine gun. Below the main bridge was an emergency steering house, which was entirely enclosed in concrete. There was a small opening at the front and when one was at the helm in convoy all one could see was a tiny part of the bow of the ship and the ship ahead of us. A speaking tube led down from the main bridge to the helmsman below, allowing the officer of the watch on the bridge above to relay his orders about alterations of course to the helmsman. During the attack I was ordered to take over this emergency helm and as I stood at there I could hear the scream of bombs outside. Suddenly I heard one come hurtling down and I was sure it was coming in beside me. I left the helm and dived outside to have a look, just in time to see a plane explode above us. I became so interested that for a couple of minutes I forgot that I was supposed to be steering the ship. On remembering, I dived back inside to hear an angry voice shouting down the speaking tube. It was the Captain. I identified myself and the reply came back, "I don't mind you writing your name all over the

Mediterranean, but I do mind when you turn back to dot the bloody i's."
While I had been away from the helm the ship had been swinging about
all over the place.

Our fuel was nearly finished and we were almost in sight of Valetta
harbour in Malta when we were ordered back to Gibraltar. This was the
most dangerous part of our journey as we had to return alone. In convoy
one always felt the companionship of the other ships, but sailing alone
made one feel like a sitting duck, easy prey for plane or U-boat. It was a
great relief to eventually see the tip of the great rock rise from the mist
ahead.   At least we would be safe for the next couple of weeks, until we
sailed on our next convoy down the Med.

While we lay in Gibraltar we were used as a depot ship. Tankers
pumped oil into us and then we in turn fuelled destroyers. This was a
twenty-four hour a day operation so we were kept on seagoing watches,
which consisted of four hours on duty and eight hours off duty. I have
known us to have as many as four destroyers alongside us at the same
time, two on our port side and two on our starboard side. I think we
knew the name of every destroyer, sloop and corvette in the Med and
many a famous name there was amongst them. We also got to know
their crews and often swapped yarns on the subject of the great Battle
of the Atlantic.

On returning to Gibraltar following that first convoy Jack and
I received cheques for the wages owed to us by the company which
had owned the ship on which we were torpedoed. Accompanying
the cheques was a statement of account containing two items which
amused me. One stated that the minute we were torpedoed our
war bonus, or danger money as we called it, was halved. I would
have thought that the days we spent on the lifeboat were even more
dangerous than those spent aboard ship. However this was the rule
for all Merchant seamen. The other item referred to loss of effects, for
which the maximum payment was fifteen pounds. Few ever received
this however; most, like myself, were awarded the minimum sum of
ten pounds. It would be the last time I would take my dinner suit
aboard a tramp steamer.

While we were stationed in Gibraltar we were issued with permits which allowed us to cross the border into Spain. One had to cross back from the Spanish side of the border no later than 9 pm, otherwise one could find oneself thrown into a Spanish prison and classed as a political prisoner. It could take months before one's release was secured. On the Gibraltar side of the frontier there was a 10 pm curfew which meant that all civilians had to be off the streets by that time. If anyone was caught out after curfew he was put in jail for the night and provided he could satisfy the authorities that he was not an enemy agent, he was given a cup of tea in the morning and released at 6 am after being fined one pound. I enjoyed this hospitality on a few occasions during my stay in Gibraltar.

One night when Jack and I had crossed the border into Spain Jack wandered off. As the time drew near for us to re-cross the frontier I became worried about him. I searched around and eventually found him slumped across a table in a bar, dead drunk. I slung him over my shoulder and staggered across the frontier. We made it with only minutes to spare and as soon as my feet touched the other side of the border I dumped my burden. I was exhausted and could carry him no further. As I could not leave him there alone I settled down beside him and waited for the police to pick us up and put us in jail, which they duly did. The following morning Jack was very happy to pay up two pounds. It was cheap compared to what would have happened across the border.

On one occasion a Catalina flying boat caught fire while tied up at its moorings in Gibraltar harbour. It was towed out of the harbour and sunk in the Straits. Next day the Germans claimed that one of their frogmen had managed to enter the harbour and had blown up a cruiser. To give the Germans some credit they did indeed manage to get frogmen through the massive defence system on at least one occasion, which was an amazing feat. However I believe they were captured before they did much damage.

Another night the Germans sent over fifty or more planes to bomb Gibraltar. There was no blackout there, presumably because Spain, being neutral, was fully illuminated. From the air at night therefore, it was hard to distinguish Gibraltar from Spain. As the bombers flew overhead the Gibraltan guns did not open fire and we had a ringside seat as we watched all the bombs fall on Spain. As the bombers flew back empty over Gibraltar every gun on the rock opened fire. It was the loudest barrage I had ever heard. I am sure Goering had few kind words for those embarrassed pilots on their return to base.

We made a couple of runs down the Med on our own, not going anywhere in particular. At night, destroyers would appear out of the darkness, then after fuelling, slip back into the murk. It all seemed rather strange to us. Later we learned that they were a section called the Moonlight Commandoes, who were carrying out some operations prior to the North African invasion, which now seemed to be imminent.

As we refuelled at Gibraltar a huge convoy began to form out in the Straits. Each day it grew larger and larger as more and more ships came in from the Atlantic. There was every conceivable type of ship: landing craft, aircraft carriers, destroyers, heavy and light cruisers, supply ships and all kinds of Merchant ships. It seemed that all the ships on the seas had been ordered to gather in the Straits of Gibraltar. This was no ordinary convoy.

As we lay there waiting for orders to sail, we speculated on what it was all about. Rumour had been rife on the Rock for some time that Operation Torch[9], or the invasion of North Africa, was about to begin. We realised that this was it and as I lay on my bunk I thought what a bloody fool I was to be here when I should have been home in Britain.

At last the orders to get underway were given. All around us was hustle and bustle as the huge armada got underway. As usual we were placed at the back of one of the columns to allow easy access for fuelling. I looked

---

9 Operation Torch was the British-American invasion of French North Africa during the North African Campaign of the Second World War which started on 8 November 1942.

around and all I could see was ships. I could not help but feel proud that I was part of something which would go down in history, ironically a subject which I had hated at school. I looked at the great transporters around me, packed with thousands of troops and I wondered how many of us would still be alive in a few days' time, for I was convinced that the Germans must already know that we were coming and would blast us out of the water with their long range artillery.

We sailed down the North African coast and parts of the invasion forces detached themselves from the main convoy as we passed Oran,[10] Algiers, Philipville[11]. I saw the invasion barges head in towards the coast and I felt great admiration for the troops in them. We had been so engaged with the war at sea that we had almost forgotten we had an army and air force fighting just as bitterly on land and in the air.

I followed the course of the invasion barges as they ran on to the beaches through powerful naval binoculars, and there were two barges in particular which drew my attention. I could have sworn I saw sheep emerging from them, but I thought my eyes were deceiving me. Later I heard that sheep had been used to explode the various booby traps and mines ahead of the troops – better that sheep died than men.

Eventually we arrived at a place called Bougie[12]. This was as far as our ship was going as our fuel for the destroyers was all used up. Now we would return to Gibraltar. As we lay off Bougie, however, awaiting orders, all hell was let loose. On the horizon we could see gun flashes and seconds later we heard the scream of shells as they passed over us, followed by explosions in the hills above Bougie as they sought out their targets. Then we saw the flash of the German artillery up there in the hills as they replied. It was mighty uncomfortable for us, for we were

---

10   Oran is Algeria's second most important city after the capital Algiers and lies on the Mediterranean Sea coast at the point where Algeria is closest to Spain.

11   Now known as Skikda, it is situated on the Gulf of Stora, north-east Algeria.

12   Now Béjaïa, it lies on the Gulf of Béjaïa, north-east Algeria.

lying in the cross-fire and were within range of the German artillery. We heard later that the *Rodney* and *Nelson* had been shelling the German gun emplacement from about ten miles out.

At last we were told to return to Gibraltar and so, at full speed, we began a zigzag course out of Bougie. I believe some gunnery officer up in those hills decided to have a bit of target practice on us, for as we wove our way out of range, shells burst to port, starboard and ahead of us. Still, we made it back to the safety of Gibraltar harbour, although I did feel rather disappointed that I had not set foot in North Africa.

After another couple of trips down to Alexandria[13] and still never having set foot ashore, Jack and I returned to Gibraltar to find that our reliefs had arrived. We packed the few bits and pieces we had accumulated and boarded the troopship which had been detailed to take us home. That evening we headed down the Med, but as soon as it became dark we about turned and headed far out into the Atlantic. This was to fool any German agent who might have been watching our departure.

The troopship on which we were sailing was of some twenty five thousand tons with a speed in excess of twenty knots, therefore we sailed alone. In peacetime she had been a luxury liner, taking the rich to the lands of sunshine. Now she was stripped of all luxury. On board we had about six thousand souls; four thousand troops and the rest mostly refugees. There were Poles, Norwegians, Belgians, French Foreign Legion, Merchant seamen like myself and quite a few Wrens who were going home a lot stouter than they had left.

The voyage home was uneventful and most of our time was taken up with boat drill. My station happened to be a gigantic raft weighing all of a ton, which lay up on the quarter deck. There were about thirty of us round it during drill one day when a young army officer approached me, looking rather puzzled.

"How would we launch this bloody thing if the ship was sinking?" he asked.

---

13 Alexandria is Egypt's largest seaport and second largest city.

"You don't," I replied, "You sit in it and wait until the ship goes down far enough to float it." That poor officer looked very seasick.

As we tied up in Liverpool I thought that it certainly was a strange world. I had left Britain to go to the River Plate. Here I was back home and though I had not been to the Plate, it had certainly been an eventful voyage. How many more voyages would I make and still survive to remember them?

Jack and I reported to the shipping office in Liverpool where we were given all the money due to us. This amounted to about one hundred and twenty pounds each which, at that time, was quite a tidy sum. We were also given railway passes allowing us to travel wherever we wished to spend our leave, which would be of six weeks' duration, for we were still due our month's survivor's leave.

We made our way to a bar in Lime Street where we both got well and truly drunk. I remember Jack saying something about going to Grimsby. Suddenly he disappeared and I never saw him again. We had been through all hell together and had become very fond of each other. We had so much in common; no homes, no families. We were just a couple of wanderers on the seas of the world. Knowing Jack as I did, I understood that he had deliberately departed that way. He was a hard old fellow and it would not have done if he had shown weakness at parting. Perhaps he would be blown to bits on his next ship. So for that matter might I, but that was the price of war. In the meantime I had leave and money in my pocket. To hell with the war – it could wait.

I booked into a first class hotel in Lime Street and for the next ten days lived like a lord. I enjoyed wine, women and song and why not? I had always made it a rule that when my money was finished then so was my leave. I never remember my money outlasting my leave and so, after ten days, I had to leave my plush hotel and move into one of the many sailors' homes which dotted the docks area of Liverpool. Within another week I was broke but happy. I had enjoyed myself and besides, if anything did happen to me, I had no one to whom I could leave any money. I did not even have to worry about funeral expenses. The sea had plenty of room.

My next voyage took me across to Boston. It was now 1943 and I was twenty years old. Though at that time we did not know it, this was the year of decision in the Battle of the Atlantic. Our new techniques of hunting down and destroying the U-boats were beginning to have results. For the first time since the war started the battle was turning in our favour. No longer could the U-boats penetrate the escorting destroyers, enter the heart of the convoy to pick out their victims, then slip away with comparative ease. Like cornered rats they fought back with terrible ferocity and although the losses of U-boats mounted, so too did the losses of British ships and men. The battle had now reached its full fury. No quarter was asked or given by either side. These were the conditions I faced as we left Boston and made for Halifax, Nova Scotia. On the convoy out we had suffered heavy losses as the U-boats no longer waited until we were homeward bound, but attacked the convoy in packs.

As we headed out into the stormy North Atlantic I again wondered how many of these proud ships would make it home. I did not have to wonder for long. Almost immediately the attacks started and I watched the now familiar sight of ships blazing and sinking. The convoy was being attacked on both flanks. Torpedoes streaked the sea from both port and starboard but it seemed as if they were being fired at random, for few of them appeared to be aimed at any particular target. It was more by luck than judgement that they struck. The escorts now had a new method of defence. In the early days they went off to chase the U-boats, which left the convoy exposed. Now only two or three left the convoy to do the hunting, while the rest ringed the convoy, dropping depth charges.

In this particular convoy we had what was known as a rescue ship, whose job it was to stop and pick up survivors. Unlike a hospital ship there was nothing to distinguish her from the other ships in the convoy. About three to four hundred miles west of Ireland she was struck by a torpedo and went to the bottom in minutes. Many men must have gone down with her, for she had been picking up survivors all the time. Probably a good number of those men had been helpless, having been wounded when their own ships had sunk, but I in no way blamed the U-boat which had struck her, for I believe that if he had known her business it would not have happened. It may sound strange, but I held no bitterness against the U-boat crews. On the contrary, I could not help admiring their skill and daring, for they continued to press home their attacks with utter disregard for their own safety, against overwhelming odds. Perhaps I was fortunate but never did I observe any acts of atrocity carried out by U-boats. They had their job to do and we had ours. The rules of war are bitter.

Outwardly, I must have appeared hard and perhaps a little cruel to my mates in the convoys. When we were under attack some men showed their fear and I mocked them. But I was frightened too. I did not tell them about my fearful nightmares. In my dream our lifeboat had turned over and as I was struggling in the sea a great fin would appear and suddenly my legs would go numb. But it was only a poor African stoker who had died, straddled across them. I never told them either of the loneliness I felt as I watched them write to or read letters from the people who loved and cared for them.

A third time I found myself heading out across the Atlantic, this time heading for St Johns, New Brunswick, before leaving Halifax in convoy for home. This time we were more fortunate, for the weather and seas were too stormy for the U-boats to attack. Halfway home however the seas calmed. The U-boats had been dogging our trail, waiting for a break in the weather. A big Merchantman, to port of us in the column, was hit and she immediately keeled over. The crew, with no time to launch the lifeboats, began to jump overboard and were kept afloat by their life-jackets. A destroyer headed towards them at slow speed, we assumed with the intention of picking them up. Suddenly though, her bow wave rose high as she increased speed and to our horror, she headed at full throttle through the patch of water containing those bobbing dots. Then, to add to our dismay, an underwater explosion of depth charges vibrated through the convoy. The destroyer passed on through the lines of ships and the patch of water became smooth again.

The bobbing dots had disappeared. The destroyer turned, came back again and repeated the pattern. We never knew if she got the U-boat. We felt numb with shock, but my heart went out to the Commander of that destroyer. It had been a case of sacrificing a few so that many might live, for there was no doubt whatsoever that the U-boat had been below those survivors. What a terrible dilemma. How many of us could have carried out our duty under such circumstances?

Between voyages I did all the things that sailors do. I must have drunk in some of the toughest dockside pubs in Britain. I can remember, on two occasions, as I made my way back to my ship through the blacked out, lonely docks, being set upon by dockside thugs. However I had sailed with some of the hardest firemen in Glasgow and Liverpool and I was well trained to look after myself. I knew what it was to take a beating, but I had also learned how to hand one out.

After one leave which I had decided to spend in Bristol, I reported for duty and was given a ship sailing from that port. She was an old tramp steamer and I was delighted to learn that our destination was Lisbon. This time I would really enjoy myself, for besides knowing the city well, I would have money to spend. When I heard the nature of our cargo however, I had grave doubts that I would ever see Lisbon again, or anywhere else for that matter. The cargo was ammunition, the deadliest of all. I had watched ammunition ships blow up. I remembered the last one I had seen. There had been a brilliant orange flash about fifty feet above the sea, rising to at least a hundred and fifty feet, followed by a sudden blast of hot wind which roared through the convoy, and then, in seconds, nothing – nothing but a terrible silence; the silence of all eternity. The human mind was unable to grasp that it had all really happened until the shocked brain began to absorb the sight of the small pieces of wreckage scattered around the convoy. A proud ship and at least fifty brave lives were wiped out in seconds.

The reason we were taking the ammunition to Lisbon was that Portugal had leased us an air strip in the Azores and we, in turn, were assisting them to mobilise their army. We sailed in convoy and as usual, found ourselves placed at the rear of one of the columns. Everything went smoothly until the third evening, when the chief engineer came up to the bridge. He and the Captain spoke together. It turned out that there was something wrong in the engine room, which meant that we would have to drop out of the convoy to carry out the necessary repair. We notified the commodore ship of our plight. He signalled back that he would detail a corvette to stay with us until our repair was completed, then he wished us good luck and Godspeed. We certainly needed both. We slowly dropped back and eventually stopped. The convoy drew further and further away and finally disappeared over the horizon, leaving us a sitting duck in the middle of the ocean, with enough explosives to blow up a city.

The engineers got to work down below. They had to use heavy sledgehammers and this made matters worse, as sound travels for many miles under water. To add to our problems, as night drew in a full moon rose and seemed to light up the whole sea for miles around us. The corvette slowly circled us at a very respectable distance. Every now and again she came in close enough to hail us and enquired how much bloody longer we would be. On one occasion, when it seemed the engineers below were running amok with their hammers and the hull of our ship rang like a bell, the corvette closed in.

"You crowd of crazy bastards! Can't you make less noise? Even Hitler in Berlin is complaining that he cannot get to sleep."

"If you bloody weekend sailors think you can do any better you are very welcome aboard," we retorted. This type of chit-chat between us was the language of the sea. There was no offence meant and none taken. We had too much respect for each other to really mean such childish remarks.

That night, as I crouched in the machine gun nest, I felt very tense, as did everyone else. Every clang of those hammers sent the cold sweat of fear running down my back. I began to imagine that we were surrounded by U-boats, waiting and watching just as a cat watches a mouse, ready to deliver the death blow. I thought of those engineers below, working stripped to the waist in the dim light of the engine room, their bodies glistening with sweat as they toiled in the humid heat. They also knew only too well the terrible danger we were in every time they swung those cursed hammers.

My mind drifted back to my little island, and I thought of my home, which would be lying dark and desolate now. I looked up at that damned moon. How I hated it that night and yet, gazing at it, my mind went back to my boyhood days when that same moon bathed my island with a rare beauty. In my mind's eye I could see black shadows flit across the fields as a cloud crossed across the moon's face, and then, once the cloud passed, the small, white-washed cottages become visible, glowing in the distance. Oh, how my heart longed to be there, away from this world of death and destruction. Perhaps someday this terrible war would end and maybe, just maybe, I would again stroll down the white, dusty roads of my childhood. I had had some close shaves with death over the last three and a half years but perhaps my guardian angel would let me see another sunrise. Sure enough, as the cold, grey streaks of dawn appeared across the sky, the magic words, sounding like a choir of angels, came from the engine room, "Job complete. Let's get the hell out of here." At least we had survived to see another day.

We notified the corvette and headed south. We were about twenty-four hours steaming from Lisbon. The convoy was now some eighty miles ahead of us and it was useless to even think of catching up with it. So, with our faithful escort, we steamed on.

That afternoon, as I lay on my bunk listening to the steady throb of the engines, I loosened the strings of my life-jacket and tried to make myself more comfortable. This was rather difficult as I was fully clothed, but in those days it was not unusual for one to go to one's bunk in this state for several days, sometimes without even removing one's sea boots.

In fact, in some ships in which I had sailed, I had seldom found the time to wash or shave during the long days and nights at sea. The smell of human sweat in the foc'sle sometimes became a bit overpowering. It was not that we were too lazy to wash, but after being under attack for hours or even days on end, personal hygiene took second place to snatching a few hours' sleep. As I lay on my bunk, thinking of these things, I began to doze. Then, somewhere in the distance, I realised I could hear a bell ringing. Still dazed with sleep, I automatically swung my legs over the bunk, simultaneously tying up my life-jacket. Reaching for my steel helmet, I raced along the deck to my machine gun post on the poop deck at the stern of the ship.

Apparently the corvette had signalled us to tell us that the convoy ahead had been attacked by enemy aircraft, which were now heading in our direction. I strapped myself into the Oerlikon and pointed it towards the sky in the direction from which they would come. As I leant back, rubbing the sleep from my eyes and scanning the clear, blue sky, I could not help but think how very tired I felt. I just wanted to close my eyes and go to sleep. These may seem strange thoughts at such a time, but the need for sleep becomes so overpowering that nothing else, not even death, really matters.

The minutes ticked past and still nothing appeared to disturb the calmness of the sky. The waiting was always the worst part. My hands clutched the grips of the gun until they became numb. Perspiration ran into my eyes and burned them. My dry tongue licked my equally dry lips and tasted the bitterness of salt from my sweat; the sweat of fear and tension. Then, with blessed relief, I heard the familiar drone of approaching aircraft.

As I gazed in the direction of the sound, I picked out three small specks. Closer and closer they came until I identified them as long range Focke-Wulf bombers. They were flying in tight formation and were very high, well out of range of our guns. As they approached one dropped height, but was still too high for a bombing run. The corvette opened fire but it was only a token gesture. They passed directly over us and as they did so I was horrified to see a stick of bombs fall from the lowest aircraft. To me, it looked as if the bombs were headed straight for us. At that moment in time I think I must have shut my eyes. I could hear the whistle as they hurtled towards us, then an explosion. Looking astern, I watched the sea rise in a terrific twenty foot spiral of pure white spray. Two more spirals rose as another two bombs fell right in our wake. They had missed us by fractions of a second. If they had not, I would have had all the sleep I wanted. It appeared that they had used up all their bombs on the convoy and had only those three left. The corvette signalled that our aim was bloody awful, but the Germans' was not much better, thank God.

Arriving in Lisbon without further mishap, we unloaded our cargo of death, loading instead cases of sardines and huge casks of port. Strange indeed were some of the loads we carried. We spent a week in Lisbon and as the only one who had been there before, I found myself in great demand as a courier. I went back to the fish bar where Jack and I had met the two German agents. I ordered a beer and went to the same table as we had sat at that night. I stared at the empty chair which faced me for a long, long time, feeling very lonely indeed. I had known nothing in life but poverty and a war which seemed to stretch back to my childhood. My life had been a battle for survival for as long as I could remember. I came back to reality and felt angry with myself, for there was no room in my world for love or sentiment. After a week in Lisbon we left for home and arrived in Avonmouth with a few days' leave.

When I reported back to the shipping office at Avonmouth I was asked how would I like to join a nice, safe ship, one that the Germans would not sink? I did not believe such a ship existed, but it turned out to be a hospital ship, so I decided to join her. As I climbed up the gangway I looked at my new home. She consisted of some twelve thousand tons and had been a cargo passenger ship before being converted to her present role. She was painted all over with sparkling white paint and her sides carried huge red crosses. Her decks were scrubbed to spotless perfection. She carried about seventy Royal Army Medical Corps, twenty-five army nurses, each holding the rank of nursing sister, a matron and a colonel who together were in charge of all the medical staff.

She had two operating theatres and wards capable of accommodating three hundred severely wounded servicemen.

As we made ready for sea I discovered that our job was to run down the coast of North Africa to pick up the wounded and bring them home to Avonmouth, where they would be dispersed to various hospitals throughout the country. The round trip had to take us three weeks and we must sail clear of all convoy routes, reporting our exact position every hour or so, even to Germany. Before we sailed we took aboard almost two hundred young nursing sisters, to be dropped off in batches at the various ports we touched, probably to nurse in field hospitals.

After the first few days at sea I realised I was not happy on that ship. She was so completely different from the dirty old cargo ships with their battleship grey paint and their cold steel decks red and eaten by rust from the waves that continually washed over them as they ploughed through the mountainous green seas of the North Atlantic. On this ship it was all spit and polish. We washed white paintwork until we became blinded by it. There was of course boat and fire drill at least twice a day and nobody wore life-jackets because the Germans would not sink this ship. However, I felt very uneasy, for I was not so sure. We sailed down the Med as far as Port Said[14] and then, loaded with our cargo of human suffering, headed for home.

On my third trip out in this ship I ran into trouble while we were having another of our boat drills. I was utterly disgusted by the whole set-up. When the Captain and the chief officer were inspecting us the chief officer took exception to my bored attitude and in a heated exchange of words, he told me to report to the Captain's cabin immediately after drill. As a result, I found myself facing the Captain across his desk, with the chief officer in attendance to substantiate his version of the incident. The Captain gave me a good dressing down and proceeded to tell me how essential it was that we knew how to launch the boat and how to handle it once it was in the water. He asked me if I knew what it would be like to handle a lifeboat in heavy seas with frightened, inexperienced

---

14 Port Said lies on the north-east coast of Egypt, north of the Suez Canal.

people on board. I replied that I had experience of this and when he asked me where, I related the story of those long days in the lifeboat. Both the Captain and the chief officer showed great interest in what I said and in the end the chief officer withdrew the charges. As I started to leave the cabin I turned to face the Captain.

"May I ask a question, Captain?" I asked.

"Certainly," came the reply.

"How do you get three hundred stretchers into lifeboats on a fast sinking ship, especially when there are not enough lifeboats?"

"That is something we don't allow ourselves to think too much about. Anyway, with our red crosses and the Geneva Convention there is little, if any, need to worry about it," replied the Captain. I was sorry I could not share his faith in the tolerance of man for his fellow man.

On my next trip out I was promoted to Acting Quartermaster. I was delighted by this, for it meant that there would be no more scrubbing decks or washing paintwork. It also showed that the chief officer's confidence in me had been restored for, in my new position I found myself in charge of the crew and the launching of my particular lifeboat.

In the following months I got to know the coast of North Africa like the back of my hand. I used to lean over the ship's rail when we were in port and watch the stretchers being unloaded from the long lines of ambulances and carried on board by German and Italian prisoners of war. Watching those helpless, broken bodies on the stretchers, some with no legs or arms, most with at least one limb missing and some blind, I realised I was very frightened. It was a fear worse than any I had ever known. It was not fear *for* myself but *of* myself. I had nightmares about the ship going down and those helpless men lying in the wards below with no chance of being saved. I wondered how I would react when faced with the terrible dilemma of deciding whether to stay and drown with them or to save myself and live the rest of my life wishing I had died with them.

At the end of my six month contract I left the ship and as I walked down the gangway, I had mixed feelings. Perhaps I was running away from my fear. My mother's words were ringing in my head, "There is no shame in fear, only in giving in to it." That nice, safe ship was the one on which I had felt most fear. I had a premonition that sooner or later, something was going to happen to her, but at least I would not be there to have to make that terrible decision.

I decided to go back to Glasgow to spend my leave. Most of it I spent between the pools office and the many tough dockside bars. I went anywhere I could be among seamen. They were the men I understood and those were the places I could find them. I began to notice that many of the old familiar faces were missing and when I inquired about them I was told, on most occasions, that they had been lost at sea. A new breed of seamen was beginning to frequent the pools office, many of them following in their fathers' footsteps, and probably many of them would perish as their fathers had done before them.

As I drank in those dockside bars I studied those young men. Though most were around my age, I felt so much older than them. In fact I felt that I had been around for an awfully long time. I listened to them eagerly discussing the war at sea. They were obviously enjoying it. They reminded me so much of myself in those early months of the war, when I had felt that it was all a great adventure, just as they did now. No wonder I felt that I had been around forever.

Some time later I heard that the hospital ship had been bombed and sunk in the Med near Italy. The Germans denied it at first, but later claimed that it had happened by accident. Then they declared that the sinking was carried out in retaliation for one of their ships which we had sunk. I never learned the true circumstances, or whether it happened before she was loaded, or what loss of life there was. All that I knew was that I had not had to make that decision.

Chapter Ten

Dancing with Ella

When my leave was finished I reported back to the Glasgow pool, where I was given a coastal vessel. I was pleased to accept as I had been thinking of going back on the coast for a spell. The vessel to which I was assigned was general cargo and would be trading, for the most part, around the ports of England, many of which I knew from the early days. It would make a change from the coast of North Africa, a part of the world of which I had seen enough.

It was now 1944 and the war was being won by the Allies on all fronts, including the Battle of the Atlantic. U-boats were on the defensive and were being lost faster than they could be replaced. Our new devices – especially radar – gave them very little chance of success. The question now was not would we win the war but rather, how long would it take us to do so? Germany however, was not going to accept defeat too easily. She still had a trump card to play.

Radar had played a large part in reducing the heavy air raid attacks, supported by a much improved ack-ack system and of course, the brilliance and bravery of our fighter pilots. The Germans were finding it too costly to maintain their heavy air raids over the south of England. It looked as if we had them beaten in the skies too.

To our horror however, rockets began to rain down on the cities and towns of southern England. We could hear and see them as they streaked across the sky, but it seemed there was no defence against them. Gradually our fighter pilots began to get to grips with the problem. It became an everyday occurrence to hear the rat-tat of machine gun fire and on looking up, one would see a spitfire chasing a V-1 rocket, as they were known, across the sky, with its machine guns blazing away. There would be a flash and that was another rocket blown up in the air. The RAF became so successful at this game that we almost had it mastered – until the day that a new type of rocket, known as a V-2, arrived and against this we had no defence. They were damnable weapons of destruction. There was no system of warning and the first one knew of their arrival was the explosion around one. They rained from the sky day and night causing terrible damage and loss of life. If Germany had perfected them sooner the outcome of the war might have been very different.

Life at sea, in coastal waters, had not changed much. However the war had changed me. These four years, with death as my constant companion, were beginning to take their toll. I was becoming jumpy and nervous and I started to drink heavily. What else was there to do? It helped me to forget out the sight of ships blazing, their bows rearing out of the sea like great tombstones, then sliding out of sight to the depths below. It helped to erase the memory of a blazing tanker, its crew trapped like rats and the sight of those bobbing, human dots with a knife-sharp bow bearing down on them. On top of all these things, there was a feeling of great loneliness and yearning in my heart for something I could not understand.

My loneliness did not mean that I was a lone wolf for I was seldom, if ever, ashore on my own. In fact, I was popular with all my mates and a crowd of us always went ashore together. This happened on every ship I sailed on, but a man can feel alone even in a crowd without knowing why. I had met lots of girls as most sailors do. I had liked a few, but nothing more.

Due to the nature of the work I was able to spend more time ashore than in recent years. One night I made my way down the blacked out docks in Cardiff, towards my ship. She was lying at the coaling berth, for we had been taking on coal for the ship's furnaces. The water in the dock basin had been raised until it was almost level with the quayside. To complicate matters, there was a film of coal dust on the water and the dockside so that, even in daylight, it was difficult to distinguish between the quay and the water. At night, in the black-out, it was impossible. I took a step and found myself plunging into the freezing water. I thought my lungs would burst. At last I came up and gasped some air into my tortured lungs before sinking again.

I popped up again, clutching desperately at the side of the dock, but it was slippery with slime. To make matters worse I had never learned to swim. Each time I rose to the surface I shouted for help before going down again. At last an old railway shunter and a member of the Home Guard heard my cries and managed eventually to pull me out, more dead than alive. A week later I was still coughing up coal dust. On reflection I felt that it would be rather ironic had I drowned in a Cardiff dock after surviving those many thousands of miles of U-boat infested seas. Sadly many seamen were drowned while making their way down those, dark quaysides.

Another night I found myself in the Elephant and Castle area of London. It was a cold, dismal night with heavy rain and I was walking along with my coat collar turned up and my head bowed. The street was deserted due to the lateness of the hour and the inclement weather. Suddenly there was a blinding flash, followed by a terrific explosion and I was swept up like a straw and hurled through a plate glass window. I got to my feet and looked around me in a daze. In the glow of the flames, to my horror, I could distinguish dead bodies lying all around me. I quickly made my way through the window into the blazing street and looked back at the shop in which I had found myself. There, above the window, were the remaining letters of the name of a well-known British tailor. The 'bodies' were tailor's dummies. I felt very shocked and shaken but other than that, I had not suffered so much as a scratch. Perhaps the window had given way with the blast and I had only been blown through the opening. It showed how suddenly death came from the sky, with no warning. These V-2 rockets were pure hell.

The bitterest memory of all was of a day in London when, in broad daylight, a V-2 had fallen in a street near Commercial Road, in the dock area. There was a heavy loss of life. The rescue workers pulled bodies from the rubble and laid them out in the street. It was believed that some people might still be alive underneath so we did not wait to be asked to assist. I found myself pulling at the rubble with the rest. I helped to carry one old lady aged between sixty and seventy and we laid her down beside the other bodies, her purse and her ration book still clutched tightly in her hand.

Very occasionally there were lighter moments, for instance the time a friend and I decided to go to a restaurant. It was a workers' place, full of dockers and lorry drivers. As we sat down at a table there was suddenly a terrible vibration and the crockery on the tables began to dance about. My friend and I looked at each other and took a dive under the nearest table. The vibration finally died away and, as we peered out from beneath the table, we were surprised to find everyone looking at us as if we were mad. Sheepishly we tried to explain that we had thought it was a bomb. At this there were tears of laughter. We joined in when it was explained that the restaurant was built into a railway embankment and trains passed over the top.

Life on those little coasters was really rough however. We were issued with a Merchant navy ration book which entitled us to more than the ordinary ration book did and in port we got time off to do our shopping. We were supposed to cook our meals at sea during our watch off, however many of us spent most of our money on other things and found ourselves with little left to buy food. Often I spent a week at sea with little more than a loaf of bread, some cans of beans and of course, the old faithful, a couple of tins of horrible dried egg powder. We used to mix the egg powder with a little water and put it into the frying pan. It puffed up into a beautiful omelette, but when we took it from the pan it collapsed, leaving us with an unappetising rubbery substance. However it filled an empty stomach. Some of the dishes we concocted in those days were weird and wonderful indeed.

Added to these hazards was of course the problem of the elements. In shallow coastal waters a ship behaves in a very different manner from the way she behaves when sailing in the deep waters of the Atlantic. There, in the long, slow swell, the ship rises and falls with a regular rhythm, but on the coast, with its many cross currents, the small ships rolled and dived, all at the same time. We called it the corkscrew motion. Trying to walk along the deck was like trying to ride a bucking bronco in a cowboy film. Many a man who had sailed deep-sea all his life found himself seasick when he sailed on the coasters.

After a few months on the coast I decided to go deep-sea again. At least there I would get my food supplied; that is if one could call it food. Prisoners in jail were served with better food than I was on some ships. Another point in favour of deep-sea was the fact that, owing to the long days at sea, I always had some money. On the coast, with regular calls at ports, I spent my money faster than I earned it. All these things considered, I made my way to the pools office in Glasgow. I walked across the George V Bridge which spans the Clyde and I saw a familiar figure walking towards me. As we drew closer I recognised Kenny, who had sailed with me on my first ship when I was a galley boy. It was a wonderful reunion after such a long time. He was very surprised to see me as he had heard that I had been lost at sea. He told me that he was now married to Jessie, the girl he had been taking out when I had last seen him, and they had a son. I mentioned my intention of going back to deep-sea, but he told me that he was still sailing with the same shipping line and there was a vacancy on his ship. After a bit of persuasion I decided to join him back on the coast.

I found myself back on the old run which I had known so well in those far off, peacetime days. Over the following weeks my old shipmate kept suggesting that I come home with him to meet his wife and son. I promised I would but, alas, each time, I set off with good intentions only to end up drinking in a bar until closing time. The war and alcohol were enclosing me in an ever tightening web.

At last, when we docked one evening two months later, Kenny insisted on escorting me to his home before I had time to reach a bar. I walked into his house and it all seemed so strange to me – the wallpaper, the carpets, the fire burning in the fireplace. Then it struck me that I had not been in a house for a very long time. I felt almost as I had done that day when I stepped out of Buchanan Street Station.

Gradually it dawned on me that the room was full of people. I glanced around and there she stood, looking across at me. Our eyes met and I knew at that moment that this was what my heart had been searching for. I was taken by my host and introduced to the people around me, but I could not wait to meet the girl across the room. At last I stood before her and my host told me that she was his sister-in-law. She offered her hand and said, "How do you do? I have heard so much about you that I feel as if I know you already."

I stood there holding that small, soft hand and looking into her big, brown eyes and there was no one else in the room. There was no one else in the world but her. I felt as if I was suspended from a star, with the carpet a rainbow. It was a moment of time that mere words cannot describe. Then, as if from another planet, a voice broke through that magic moment and asked us to be seated at the table.

I felt very awkward and clumsy at the table, with its snowy white tablecloth and sparkling cutlery. The china cups seemed too small and fragile for my hard, rough hands. I had become so accustomed to long wooden tables and thick pint-mugs of tea that I had forgotten there were still such things as china cups and tablecloths. My hostess served us with curry and rice, saying she had made it especially for me, remembering how fond of it I used to be. She was not to know that during those months in Gibraltar I had practically lived on the stuff and was now sick of the sight of it.

At the end of the evening I offered to escort this wonderful girl to her home. I now knew that her name was Ella and as we walked down the street together we chatted as if we had known each other all our lives. She told me that she had a boyfriend but it wasn't serious. She was very fond of dancing and preferred men who were good dancers. After I had assured her that I was a very good dancer I made a date to take her dancing the following evening.

I made my way back to the ship through the shabby back streets lined with crumbling grey tenement slums, down to the cold darkness of the lonely docks which had become so much a part of my life, but I realised my dismal surroundings had taken on a strange beauty of which I had never before been aware. My heart was singing and my loneliness had gone. I, the rough sailor who could swear with the worst of them, who had drunk in some of the toughest dives in some of the world's roughest waterfronts, was in love with a girl I had only just met.

The following day seemed endless. I thought the evening would never arrive. There was one small shadow on my happiness however; I had lied when I told her that I was a good dancer. In truth I was born left handed and, it seemed, also with two left feet, which would not do what I wanted them to do on a dancefloor. How would she react when she found out?

At last it was time to keep my date. I began to feel very nervous. What if she did not come? As I approached our arranged meeting place however, my heart jumped for joy, for there she was. We moved out on to the floor for our first dance but I was so nervous that I was even worse than usual. I kept getting out of step and having to apologise for standing on her feet. We finished the first dance and she tactfully suggested that, as the floor was very crowded, we should sit down and get to know each other over a coffee. Later, when we recalled that first date, she told me how surprised she had been when she discovered that I was not a good dancer, for she had reckoned she could tell one by looking at him. She had certainly been proved wrong by me. She told me, however, that it did not make a bit of difference as she had been in love with me from the moment our eyes had met.

My ship was in Glasgow for the next ten days for an overhaul and I dated Ella for every one of those nights. They were such wonderful evenings. The war, with all its death and destruction, was forgotten, although one night I was reminded of it in a very peculiar way.

We were sitting together on the Glasgow subway on our way to see a film. As those who have travelled on Glasgow's underground railway will know, the seats face each other down the length of each coach. The train was rushing through a tunnel but I had the impression that I was back in the lifeboat and that the people sitting opposite me were my shipmates. As we rocked and swayed I could see again those green mountains of water towering above us, ready to crash down and sweep us all to eternity. The man sitting opposite me was saying, "A brown ale for the missus, Jack, and the usual for me."

A hand pulled at my arm and a voice from faraway said, "Are you all right? Are you all right?" I came to my senses and realised that it was Ella who was speaking to me. I was shaking and a cold, damp sweat poured from me. The people opposite were staring; probably many of them thought that I had been drinking. I felt so embarrassed that we alighted at the next station even though we still had two stations to travel.

After leaving the station we decided to walk the rest of the way. Knowing that I owed Ella an explanation for my strange behaviour, I related the story of those sixteen days in the lifeboat and I explained how, over the last few months, I had been becoming more and more jumpy. She listened to me and made me promise to see a doctor the following day.

Next morning I faced the doctor across his desk. I explained the reason for my visit and told him about some of my experiences and of my many escapes. He listened with great interest and then reassured me that there was nothing physically or mentally wrong with me, before going on to explain that I was suffering from a form of shell shock. In my case the years of tension were shattering my nerves. What I needed was a few months' rest. He said that he would give me a letter to give to the Federation doctor at the pool to this effect. I pleaded with him not to do that, arguing that as I had been in the war since the beginning and that as it was obvious to everyone that it would only last a few more months, after surviving this far I wanted to see it through. Perhaps the real reason was that the sea was my life. I knew no other.

"Alright son," he replied, "I was a naval surgeon for many years and I understand exactly how you feel. All I can do for you now is wish you safe journeys."

With the knowledge that there was nothing seriously wrong with me I began to feel much better. The days flew past and the day before we were due to sail, I proposed to Ella. To my everlasting joy she accepted and we were engaged before I sailed. Within a fortnight my whole life had been transformed.

As we sailed down the coast during those final months of the war we once again heard the roar of bombers, hundreds upon hundreds of them, but this time they were our planes going over to knock hell out of the German cities. Revenge was sweet and yet I could feel nothing but compassion when I pictured those innocent German children cowering with fear as they crouched in their shelters. Why did innocent children have to suffer? It all seemed so wrong.

We no longer had U-boats to contend with and the rocket bases had been wiped out, so the biggest danger we faced at sea now was mines. They seemed to be everywhere. I think I felt more fear of being blown to bits during those last few weeks than I had over the last few years. I now had something to live for. Why should I die now?

I was lying on my bunk as we sailed up the Irish Sea towards Belfast when the news came through that the war in Europe was over. I was filled with emotion. Many times over the years I had dreamt that I would not be alive to hear that broadcast. I was twenty-two years old but I felt many years older. As I lay there my mind drifted back over those eventful years. I thought of the mates I had lost, of those two lonely graves so far away, of the convoys in which I had sailed and of those faithful watchdogs, the destroyers and the corvettes with their youthful crews who had sacrificed so much so that we and our precious cargoes might survive. I thought of the thousands of homes where the news of the end of the war would bring nothing but grief; grief for the ones who would never return. I thought of the words of our great Scottish poet, 'Man's inhumanity to man makes countless thousands mourn.' How true, how very true those words were. But for all that, it was great to be alive and even more wonderful to be loved.

Ella and I set the date for our marriage. I suddenly realised that I would have to get a copy of my birth certificate and so I wrote to the Registrar General in Edinburgh, giving what information I had. After some time I received a buff envelope. I felt quite excited as I opened it, believing that at last I would find out some details about my father. I unfolded the certificate and read its contents. I stared at it unbelievingly. There must be a mistake. I sat down and stared at the piece of paper until the truth penetrated my numb brain; I was illegitimate. What shocked me most of all however was the revelation that the woman who had struggled so hard to bring me up, the woman whose words of wisdom had such a powerful influence on my life, had not been my mother at all. My real mother's name was on that certificate but my father's, of course, was not, as she had been a widow for two years before I was born.

Nothing that had happened to me during the war had shocked me as much as the contents of that piece of paper. I felt ashamed, dirty and unclean. I was a thoroughbred, a thoroughbred bastard. I would have to break off my engagement, I thought, as I could not ask Ella to marry me now. I would go deep-sea again and sail away as far as I could.

That night I met Ella. I could not just break it off and leave her to think that I had stopped loving her. Instead I had to tell her the truth and so I showed her the birth certificate. When she had studied it she looked at me with tears in her big, brown eyes and said, "Oh, you stupid, silly man, it is you I love and if that piece of paper is part of you then I will love it too." I asked her why she was crying and she answered, "I am crying for you, for I know how terribly hurt you are and when you are hurt then so am I." I felt very ashamed of myself and I was glad that I had not told her of my plans to break off our engagement and run away. I should have known that there are some things in life which we can never run from.

I wrote to the registrar for a further check in case there had been a mistake, but there was no error. Now I knew the secret that my adoptive mother had wished to tell me that day, while we were on my favourite rock. I would never find out what my father had been like, however, I knew that the woman I had known as my mother would always be my mother.

I thought back to my childhood, searching for some word, something which would give me a clue, but I could remember nothing. Then, suddenly, I recalled something my mother had said when I was very young. Perhaps, like most young children do, I had asked her where I came from, but I could now remember her saying that she had bought me for forty pounds and that I was worth every penny of it. That might have been possible in those days, when children were sometimes given away or even sold, before illegal adoption was stopped by law.

A few weeks later Ella and I were married. We did not have a home of our own so we rented a small attic room. I used to joke that it was as near to heaven as I was likely to get, but it was indeed heaven to us. As we dreamt and planned our future together on my frequent trips home from sea, we discussed all the usual things that young married couples discuss. We tried to decide whether I should continue to go to sea or come ashore and get a job. The thought of giving up the sea made me uneasy. I knew nothing except the sea and ships. I understood the lines of a ship; I could tell just by looking at her how she would behave under certain conditions. I loved and understood the sea, its moods and its challenges. The only work I could perform ashore would be unskilled labouring and the wages would be a lot less than I was earning at sea. We discussed all these problems and decided I should come ashore. Being together was all that mattered.

Seven months after the war ended I sailed up the Clyde for the last time. As we approached our berth I watched our mooring ropes being pulled ashore and made fast. It was a scene which was second nature to me. I could smell the familiar odour that only the Clyde seemed to emit as our propeller stirred up the mud of the river bed. Many sailors loved that smell, for it meant that they were home after a long voyage. I heard the telegraph ring out 'finished with engines' and to me it meant 'finished with the sea' and the ships I loved so much. I picked up my kit bag and walked down the gangway. It occurred to me that, since this was the same shipping company with which I had started my seagoing career, it was very possibly the same gangway I had walked up as a boy. I turned and looked at the ship for the last time. I was leaving my old loves and going home to my new love.

Chapter Eleven

Life Ashore

My first job ashore was driving a crane in a huge foundry in Glasgow. It seemed like a different world from the one I had known. Having never been closed in before, I felt as if I were serving a prison sentence. I longed for the heaving decks, the salt spray stinging my face and the blue sky above me. Instead I was surrounded by rafters laden with many years' accumulation of dirt. The smell of molten metal and dust was everywhere. What windows there were in the roof were still covered with blackout paint but even without that, it was doubtful if daylight could ever have penetrated the dirt on the inside. We did not see daylight from morning to night. It was a prison indeed.

At the end of the week I took home my miserable few pounds. It was small compensation for the conditions in which we worked. After three months as a crane driver I became a trainee moulder. The work was hard, dirty and hot but the money was slightly better. I found it so difficult to settle down to the monotonous routine of life ashore, but I was determined to accept this strange new life.

One year after we were married our daughter was born and she was christened Jean. I was so happy and proud of the gifts that God had given me. I wanted to give my wife and my daughter all the good things that money could buy, but how could I, with my lack of skill? I made up my mind that what I lacked in skill I would make up for by hard work. I would chase the jobs which paid well and I would work long hours. As long as I lived, my family would never know poverty as I had known it.

With thousands of men still being demobbed it was not easy to find a job, never mind one with good wages. Even for skilled people wages were very poor. Scarcer still than jobs were houses. Glasgow had a waiting list for council housing of upwards of eighty thousand people. The city's record of tuberculosis was second only to that of Calcutta, which at the time had the highest death rate in the world from this terrible disease. I searched every factor's office in Glasgow for a house which I could rent, but it was an impossible task. I went to the Corporation housing department to put my name on the waiting list with all those other thousands of names and was told that I might hear of a house in about ten years' time.

I felt angry and frustrated by low wages and poor housing. Was this the brave new world which we had been promised? Was this what my shipmates and all the other hundreds of thousands of men and women had perished for? Perhaps it was to be a repeat performance of what had happened after the First World War. Not if I, in some small way, could help it. The question was how? I did not have much education and would have little, if any, time to improve it. But I was young and I had plenty of experience of life and even of death. I understood my fellow man, for I had seen him in hunger, in thirst, in danger and in fear. Perhaps this sort of knowledge would make up for my lack of the academic kind. Maybe I was being unfair to society; after all, we had just come through a war and it takes time to recover. But it seemed that we were too busy helping the nations we had defeated and spending too little time worrying about our own problems. I began to wonder who exactly had won the war.

In the months which followed I gave deep thought to the political machinery of our country. I also became very interested in the trade union movement and it dawned upon me that perhaps here was where I could do some good. I could at least try to improve the lot of my fellow worker in his battle for shorter working hours, paid holidays and most important of all, better wages. However, before I could even try to assist with these improvements, I would have to be elected as a shop steward. This would be no easy task as most shop stewards at that time were very much older men with many years of experience of trade union procedure behind them. They were inclined to be suspicious of young tearaways, as they called us, coming home from the war and planning to change the world overnight. To stand against these men at an election of shop stewards would be a formidable task indeed for a young, untried man, for these older men had proved themselves and were trusted by their fellow workers. However, although I had admiration and respect for the great service they had given to their respective trade unions and members, I felt it was time for young men with new ideas to take an active interest in shaping the peacetime Britain which they had fought so hard to save. With these thoughts in mind I decided to jump in at the deep end.

My voice began to be heard at union meetings, stating my opinions and putting forward motions or amendments. In those early months I suffered many defeats but I never, at any time, criticised the shop stewards, for I realised the difficult task which they were trying so hard to carry out. Gradually, more and more of my motions or amendments were carried, which meant that more people were accepting what I had to say. During our lunch breaks some debate would arise concerning the trade unions or politics and I always seemed to land in the thick of it. One day, when I was arguing about my dreams for shorter hours and better holidays, the same things that the National Executive was battling for, one old chap looked at me and shook his head.

"Since you are so bloody smart, young one, why don't you stand for shop steward at the next election?" he asked.

"Don't worry," I replied, "I will."

"You have no chance," came the reply.

I felt the same way, but I did stand at the next election. Much to my surprise I was nominated, seconded and by process of elimination, I found myself elected shop steward. I soon learned all the steps of procedure but, as a new and young steward, I found myself dealing with trivial complaints; a man swearing at a foreman for example, or a man being given an official warning. Foreman's level was as far as I was allowed to go. There was what I called the 'inner cabinet', which consisted of around six of the very experienced stewards led, of course, by the convenor, who was all-powerful and in charge of all the stewards within the factory. He of course, was responsible in turn to his full time official, but within the factory his word was law and God help any steward who overstepped procedure. This inner cabinet negotiated all the working conditions and wages with the top management, and it was where I wished to be.

My chance came sooner than I expected, for there was a 'flu epidemic when the stewards were in the middle of wage negotiations. The committee had been badly hit by the epidemic and the convenor asked me if I would sit on it. I told him that I was prepared to do so, on condition that I was not only there to make up the numbers. I wanted to express my opinions, not sit there like a dummy.

"As long as you do not contradict me or any of the other stewards you can say what you want, as long as it is constructive. If you get yourself in a corner I will cut in, and remember, when I speak you keep your mouth shut," he replied. I must have done quite well at that first meeting for the convenor congratulated me and told me that he was keeping me on the inner cabinet.

Over the following months I learned a lot through dealing with upper management. I began to realise that problems don't stop on the shop floor. Management also had their troubles, and their problems, unless solved by top management, very quickly became our problems in one way or another. Another thing which became apparent to me was that although I considered the managers to be human beings just like me, many of them did not seem to feel the same way about us. Even if they did appreciate the fact that they were only human they seemed to brush the thought aside with a feeling of, 'we are much more superior beings than you.'

A year after our daughter was born we were delighted to find a small, one-roomed flat of our own. It was so small that we had to buy a folding bed and when it was in the down position there was just no room to move about. The toilet was outside on the stairs and we shared it with the household next door. To us though, the flat was a palace. After I screwed the nameplate on the door I can remember standing back to admire it with a feeling of great happiness. No ship owner had ever felt happier at the naming of his newest ship.

Shortly afterwards I left the foundry and became a demolisher. It was hard work but the money was better and I could at least see the sky and feel the wind on my face. At this particular time we were demolishing old brick air raid shelters and we worked in teams of four men to a shelter. We reported each morning to a yard, where we boarded lorries to be driven to our particular area. One morning, as I was sitting in a lorry with my regular team, waiting for our driver who had not turned up, the foreman came along and asked me to transfer to another team for that day. Later I heard that two members of the team I should have been in had been killed when a shelter collapsed on them. My guardian angel had not forsaken me.

I changed my job many times, always looking for a bigger pay packet. Four years after my daughter was born we had another addition to the family. This time it was a son and we called him Ronald. Shortly after this we moved to a two apartment house. As if driven by a demon I worked longer and even longer hours. I took part-time jobs; at weekends I worked as a barman, a waiter and even as a bouncer in the record department of a big city store. I desperately wanted to provide well for the family I loved so dearly.

With the passing of the years my love for Ella became deeper and deeper. That magic moment when we had first met had never dimmed. We had been made for each other. She used to say to me, "I love you so much that I just know I could never live without you." She said it with such intensity that I felt quite frightened. I really did believe her for I, in turn, could not even think of the world without her.

When I came home, sometimes very late at night from my long hours of toil, I felt very, very weary. Entering my home however, was like stepping from a dark, foggy winter's night into a beautiful summer's day, with sunshine all around me. My tiredness left me as if by magic, for when we were together there was no mountain too high to climb, no problem impossible to solve. I thought back to those lonely years and wondered how I had survived them. Sometimes our deep love and dependence on each other worried me. What if it were to end in some way? When I thought of that a terrible fear which I could not explain ran over me.

Three years after my son was born another daughter arrived and she was christened Alexandra. We were delighted for now our family was complete. As the years went past I became more involved in the trade union movement and in the sometimes bitter struggle to improve the lot not only of myself and my family, but that of my fellow workers. I became a sub-convenor and attended more and more meetings and conferences.

I was so proud of my credential card and of my trade union, which I had the privilege to represent. I had long since realised that although the men trusted me as a shop steward, that in itself was not sufficient. I had to convince the management that they too, could trust me, and that once I gave my word to them, as to my members, I would never withdraw it. In this I had amazing success. I also seemed to have been given a gift in the ability to hold the undivided attention of all the management or members I addressed. I could not explain why, but I knew that it was so.

At last our names came up on the housing list and we were allocated a beautiful flat in the outskirts of Glasgow. My children could now play in green fields as once I had done, instead of on hard pavements, surrounded by sombre, grey tenements. The main attraction for the children in our new home was the bathroom and for the first few weeks they had baths twice a day. We soon began to turn the flat into the home which we had always dreamt we might have some day.

A new factory was opening near my home, so I applied for a job and was accepted. I realised that I had been spending too much time away from my family so I decided to review my position. With my new job I did not need to work such long hours and after much soul searching, I decided to give up holding office in the trade union. I would start my new job without mentioning to anyone that I had been a shop steward, not because I was ashamed, but because I knew that if the news leaked out there was a strong possibility that I might find myself talked into becoming one again. I had held this position in every place I had worked, but now I wanted to spend more time with my family. It was a hard and painful decision, for the trade union was my second love. When I began my new job I discovered that ninety-five per cent of my workmates were tradesmen and so I, as a semi-skilled man, had little or no chance of ever being elected to office anyway. I attended many meetings, fighting down the urge within me to put forward motions or amendments, but I remained silent.

Many times I had described to my family the beautiful island I had left so long ago. They often asked me when I would take them to see it. The truth was that previously I could not afford to take them, but now I could and one night I told them that we would go to Tiree for a holiday the following year. In the meantime I decided the time had come to take the plunge and buy a car, so that I could take the family to the coast and into the countryside. No Rolls Royce ever got such a welcome as that old second hand car the night I brought it home and I suppose, in my heart, no Rolls could ever take its place.

That summer we travelled all over Scotland. I had a feeling of great contentment as I watched my family play on the shores and paddle in the seas around the coast. We drove into the countryside for picnics. My family had always wanted a poodle, and so one day I came home with a beautiful little black poodle pup, who soon became one of the family. That summer was the happiest time of my life. I thanked God for the wonderful things he had bestowed on me; for my three beautiful children and for lending me one of his angels to be their mother. I loved this wonderful world. The scars of war had healed and those distant years were now shrouded in the mist of time.

The summer passed however, giving way to the coolness of autumn. One particular week in October I was on early shift. I spent the evening waxing the car in preparation for the long winter which lay ahead. By the time I finished it was almost dark. I went into the house and played with the children and the dog until they went to bed, after which the house took on that air of peacefulness that all homes assume when the children are asleep. As we always did during those peaceful hours before bedtime, Ella and I sat down by the fire with our supper and reminisced through the happy years of our marriage. We discussed the coming summer and how much we were all looking forward to seeing the island of which I had spoken so much. Then it was time for bed.

I rose the following day and prepared for my work, just like any other morning. I kissed my wife and as I stepped into my car, I looked back at her as I always did and with my usual wave I drove off. It was just another morning, or so I thought. Two hours later I received a message saying I was to go home at once. There had been an accident.

Chapter Twelve

Dark Days

Before anyone could stop me I left the factory and drove off home at high speed. My mind was reeling. What could have happened? Perhaps one of the children had been knocked down on the way to school? My mind was on everything but my driving. Suddenly I realised I was approaching a bend, a bad left hand one which I although I knew well I was heading for at double the speed at which I would usually have taken it. I slammed on the brakes, the car slewed across the road and a lamp post loomed in front of me. I pulled at the wheel and the post scraped down the side of the car.

I screeched to a halt outside my home. A crowd of people had gathered and all the windows of the house were open wide. When I burst in I saw a group of neighbours standing round somebody who was lying on the floor. The smell of burning was everywhere. I fought my way through and knelt beside the unconscious, blanket covered figure. It was Ella.

The doctor and ambulance appeared within seconds of my own arrival. The doctor ordered everyone but me out of the room and began his examination. As I looked at the injuries I felt stunned with horror. I had seen too many burn injuries from the tankers and I knew she could not survive, however my mind just would not accept that this could have happened to us.

When we arrived at the hospital the doctors made their examination, then sent for me and confirmed what I already knew. They told me that Ella's chances of survival were very slim indeed. But they were all wrong, I thought. They did not understand. She was my life – there could be no life without her. God would not take her away from us. My tortured mind tried to reason it out. Then the thought of the children came to me; they had to be comforted. I would not be able to see Ella for a couple of hours while the doctors dressed her injuries. I raced back home and found that my brother-in-law had taken the children from school and told them of the accident. I comforted them as best I could by telling them that everything would turn out alright. Somebody had taken the dog away.

It was only then that I discovered what had happened. It appeared that after seeing the children off to school, Ella's underskirt had brushed against a bar of the electric fire and she had gone up in flames. By the time the neighbours had managed to get in it was too late.

The children were taken away to stay with their uncle and aunt and the house was locked up. I returned to the hospital and sat all night by my wife's bedside, but she remained unconscious. The sister tried to reason with me, telling me to go home as there was nothing I could do, but I would not listen. I felt that as long as I was beside her Ella would not die, for I would will her to live. She just could not die and leave me and the children.

I went home to see the children for a couple of hours and then went back to the hospital to continue my lonely vigil. This routine went on for nine days. Hour after hour, day after day I sat beside her. Sometimes she opened her eyes and murmured words I could not understand.

During the nightmare of those days I prayed; oh how I prayed. I did not eat, I did not shave and I could not sleep. The sister and the nursing staff pleaded with me to go home to rest, but I just could not. I wished that I could take her place. On the ninth day she opened her eyes and this time she recognised me. In a low whisper she said, "My darling, you look so tired and you need a shave. Go home to the children. They need you. Promise me that you will always look after the children for I love you all so much. Go home, my love, and have a shave."

Before I could answer her eyes closed again. I kissed her burning cheeks and slipped away to do as she had asked. As I made my way to my sister-in-law's house I felt happier than I had in all those days. I had been right and the doctors had all been wrong. She was getting better. God had answered my prayers.

After a wash and a shave I sat down and I ate a good meal, the first in a long time. I kissed the children goodnight and reassured them that everything was going to be all right and this time I said it with conviction. I made my way back to the hospital and as I approached the ward door the sister met me. There were tears in her eyes as she told me that my wife had died just minutes earlier.

My mind was a blank over the next two days. I could not accept that she had gone from me for ever, I just could not. I seemed to live in another world. People and voices seemed to drift around me like a mountain mist. Those days were like a dream.

And so, once again, as I turned away from that same grave[15] I had turned from as a youth, my mind was filled with bitter thoughts. There was no God. How could there be? I had prayed and prayed and he had not listened. Why, oh why, was I always the one who was left? I wanted to die so that I could be with her. I just could not live without her.

For the next few days I stayed with my in-laws. Their kindness and understanding was something I would never forget. They seemed to know that in the end I would reach some decision but that, in the meantime, I wanted to be alone with my grief. The children were staying with other relatives and I did not even want to see them. At last however, I decided to go home.

For the first time since the accident I stepped into my home. I was alone, for I wanted it that way. The house was dark and silent as I sat down in a chair. How long I sat there I do not know. I looked around the home I had loved so much, picturing it as it had been, with the children fighting with each other one minute and playing the next, their mother scolding them, the little poodle running from one to the other, barking. Now there was nothing but an empty, terrible silence. I began to think about the children. The oldest girl was thirteen, the boy nine, and the youngest girl not yet six. How could I bring them up alone? It was impossible.

---

15   Alex's mother and wife were buried in the same plot.

Voices from the past hammered through my head, "Promise me you will always look after our children". My mother's voice saying, "Some day you will be a man. People will look to you for comfort, perhaps when they are afraid, or sick, or when they have lost somebody very dear to them. Give them that comfort. Never let those people down." How appropriate those words seemed now. I thought of the days in the lifeboat and of the terrible odds which faced that Captain. Our lives had depended on him. What would have happened if he had given in to the odds?

My mind was made up. I felt angry with myself for my feelings of self-pity. I had thought only of myself. What of my children? They had lost their mother and I was all they had left. Not only were they suffering from grief but also from fear, wondering what was going to happen to them. They would not have to worry any more, for they were coming home. I would bring them up and only death would separate us. Later that night I sat in my favourite chair with my youngest daughter on my knee. I told them of my plans and I could see the relief on their faces. I assured them that this would always be their home and, as far as possible, life would go on as before.

The first step was to get the children back to school and myself back to work. I brought the poodle home, but he was a mad dog now and only I could go near him. He had been in the house that tragic day. I took him to a vet who explained that there was nothing he could do as the dog's nerves were gone and so I had to have him destroyed. This meant further heartbreak for the children, but it had to be done.

Those first few weeks were the blackest of my life. I had to hide how I felt from the children. At night I heard my youngest daughter sobbing for her mother. I comforted her as best I could, but how does one comfort a child so young? Should I tell her that she would see her mother in sixty years' time in a place called heaven? I was so bitter in those early months. I hated to see other children out walking with their mothers. What had my family done to be punished? What had my wife done to deserve such a fate?

Gradually I picked up the threads of my life again, organising the shopping, the laundry, the cooking; the many tasks that go into the running of a home. I was grateful for the training I had had in my earlier years. My oldest daughter Jean became my right hand, always showing great concern for me and doing everything in her power to help. Later I discovered that the name Jean meant 'the grace of the Lord'. How true that was. The other children helped with the tasks allotted to them, and so we became a team, with each helping the others.

The months passed. They were so full of problems to be overcome that I had little time to dwell on the past, but at night, when the children were in bed, I was alone with my thoughts. Sometimes a feeling of despair gripped me and I felt I could not go on, but I had made my promise and so I must.

Slowly the tears dried on my children's cheeks. They were young and their hearts would heal. They had their friends at school and they had their home. Life was returning to normal for them. It began to look as if there was a chance of success. We were now over the worst part of it. The months stretched to years and I began to give thought again to the world around me. I needed another interest outside of the home and so once again my voice was heard at union meetings. One of my workmates had met somebody with whom I had worked many years before and the news had leaked out about my trade union activities of those earlier years. I found myself a shop steward once more and shortly after I was elected as convenor. I felt very proud of this for, though I was an unskilled man, it showed that tradesmen had confidence in my skill in other fields.

Once again my home heard the laughter of happy children. I bought another black poodle to make up for the one which had to be destroyed. At least that was something I could replace. With my work, my home and my union duties I had little, if any, time to myself. This was how I wanted it.

The years following the death of Ella were the busiest of my life, with running my home, looking after my family, working shifts and doing the numerous tasks connected with being a shop convenor. Eventually the strain began to tell on my health. It began with a feeling of exhaustion and then I began to suffer violent stomach pains. Each month at first and then each week they became worse. I was convinced I had cancer but I told no-one, not even my family. I would not go to see a doctor in case he confirmed my fears. Many times, in the grip of pain, I wanted to pray for more time to allow the children to grow older, but my bitter heart would not let me. I had prayed for Ella and what good had it done? I began to drag my legs. It seemed as if the very life was being choked from my body, but I forced myself to carry on. And so it went on for almost a year.

One night when I came home from work after being on a very dirty job, I had no strength left to wash myself. My eldest daughter had long since realised that all was not well, but I kept assuring her that I was fine. That night I went to bed just as I was, without washing. The following morning I dragged myself to work but as I entered the factory I collapsed. Fighting off the darkness that was sweeping over me, I struggled to my feet. I felt that death, that old companion, was very near, but I just couldn't die yet. I needed more time. Then a great wave of blackness swept over me and I knew no more.

For the next week my life hung by a thread. At first even the surgeons who operated held out little hope of my survival and my daughter Jean was told to expect the worst. I lay in a twilight world, unaware of the anxiety around me. During my semi-conscious moments fleeting shadows came and went and then the blackness of the darkest night surrounded me again. Somewhere in my mind I stood on the edge of a very tall chimney and on the top there were spikes. I kept losing my balance but, when I began to fall, I grabbed a spike, pulling myself back to safety.

When I grew stronger and was out of danger I was told by the surgeons that it was indeed a miracle. I had been on the operating table for about seven hours and had undergone a very major stomach operation. I was told that even for a very fit person it would have been touch and go, but in my tired and run down condition I had almost died twice during the operation.

During the weeks that followed I was given more attention than I had ever known in my life. The nursing staff were magnificent.

There was nothing they would not do for me. How does one put into words the feelings one has for such wonderful people? As I lay, propped up by pillows, I looked out of the window opposite and there, to my amazement, was a tall chimney at least a hundred feet high, topped by five spikes. Each time I pass the hospital I look up at that chimney and I remember, but the mystery will always remain with me.

Six weeks later I was sent to a convalescent home. Instead of improving however, my condition deteriorated rapidly. I went down to seven stones in weight and twelve weeks later I was back on the operating table. This time, though it was serious, death was not so close. It could never be again in one lifetime. I returned to my old ward, with the same angels of mercy nursing me back to health. Six months after I had collapsed I walked back through the factory gate, fit and ready to resume the battle of life. My guardian angel was still looking after me. I would never be as physically strong again, but I was alive.

During the months that followed I fought many battles in my capacity as convenor, but they were other people's battles and they were many and varied. One case concerned a man who had lost his wife after an illness. He began to drink heavily and his timekeeping became very bad. After many warnings he was told that he was being sacked. My committee and I swung into the defence. The management were adamant and they would not change their position. We were in deadlock. I began to berate the management for their lack of understanding of the man's position, and I finished by quoting those famous words of Robert Burns,

> *So gently scan your brother man,*
> *Still gentler sister woman,*
> *And when they gan a'daeing wrang*
> *To step aside is human.*

There was a long silence and then the man was given another chance.

In another case a man was being dismissed for striking another man at work. I had a talk with the offender to see if I could try to save him from losing his job. I asked him what had caused the incident in the first place. He told me that the other man had called him a bastard. He had taken exception to this for, as he said, he was not a bastard. I felt slightly amused, for little did he know that he was depending on one to fight for his job. This I did and he eventually received a short suspension.

Managers had changed since those earlier years when we had first come in contact. They were more flexible, more understanding and less superior. They seemed, at last, to be coming to terms with the facts of life in modern industry, realising that the power on the shop floor was as great, if not greater, than that of the boardroom and that the only way of controlling that power was to accept it.

Since being in hospital I tired more easily and was in need of a holiday and again my mind turned to my island. Again the planning started and I wrote to an old school friend, asking if we could stay with him. He replied that we would be very welcome to come to stay at his farm, so with cases packed we began the long journey.

Chapter Thirteen

Homecoming

On a lovely summer's morning the mail boat steamed out of beautiful Oban Bay, through the Sound of Mull, and out into the Minch. The early morning mist added a touch of mystery to the islands that lay around us and as it cleared, the rays of the morning sun glinted on the surface of the sea, making it sparkle and dance as if it were laughing. Out of the lingering mist ahead appeared an island, my island, the island I had dreamt of so often in those convoys of long ago. In my mind's eye, as the boat approached the pier, I could see a lonely figure waving me goodbye on a stormy winter's morning. Followed by my children, I stepped off the gangway. After thirty years I had, at last, come home.

I scanned the sea of strange faces, but none was familiar. A middle aged man stepped from the crowd.

"Excuse me," he said, in that beautiful, lilting, Highland tone, "does your name happen to be Alex?" I replied that it was. It was the friend to whom I had written. I would never have recognised him. He explained that he had known me as I was the only man to alight from the boat accompanied by two girls and a boy. He took us to his farm, where as a boy I had so often worked for his father, who had long since died.

One of the first places I visited was the site of my old house. To my astonishment the little tin house still stood there, red with rust. The windows and the door were rotting away and the weeds grew high all around it, but it was still intact after all these years. A hundred yards to the south of it lay a pile of overgrown boulders, all that was left of the byre where my mother and I had sheltered on those dark, stormy nights of so long ago. Later I was told that the little tin house was due to be demolished the following year. One could almost have thought that it had deliberately defied the elements, waiting for me to return.

The next place I visited was my old school. The gate was locked so I stood outside the old stone wall. There had been many new extensions made, but the old part remained the same. As I stood there, gazing at it, a young man emerged from the building and seeing me standing there, came over to the wall.

"Excuse me, can I help you?" he asked.

"I'm afraid you are too late," I replied. "I wish I had taken all the help I was once offered in that very same building, a long time ago." I told him part of my story. He seemed very interested and said that he would be more than pleased to show me around. I told him where my old classroom was, and he took me into it. Nothing had changed. I looked at the rows of desks and pictured the boys who had occupied them. Some were now dead, killed in the war. They too, had probably dreamt of their island but unlike me, they would never return. Their graves lay scattered over distant lands, or perhaps in the watery wastes of the cold Atlantic Ocean.

I walked through the rows of desks and sat down in the place where I used to sit. I gazed out of the window, as I used to do, and looked at the beautiful, green fields. As before, a voice broke into my thoughts. I looked up and there was my guide, watching me intently.

"You were very deep in thought. Can I ask you what you were thinking about?"

"I was thinking," I replied, "of a boy who used to sit here and dream of becoming the Captain of a great ship."

"And what happened to that boy?" asked my guide.

"Many things happened to him," I replied, "but I know he never did become the Captain of that great ship, for that boy was me." As we chatted about the school I discovered that all the old teachers had long since left. Some had died, but there was one teacher still alive and living in retirement on the island. As we were about to part, I asked my companion who the headmaster of the school was now.

"I am," he replied, with a smile.

I was determined to visit the old farm where the teacher I had once known was living. She lived alone, for her husband had long since died. Taking my children with me, I set off. As is the practice in the islands, I knocked on the door, then lifted the latch and walked in. A very old lady with pure white hair sat by the fire. She looked up as we entered, but there was no sign of recognition on her face. I pictured her as I had known her in those far off school days, and I found it hard to believe that this was the same person who had struck such terror into our hearts when we were boys.

I told her that I had once been in her class at school. She studied me intently and then her eyes strayed to my family. She studied each one of them in turn. After a long silence she looked back at me and said, "I do not recognise you, but that girl there," she said, indicating my youngest daughter, "her eyes remind me of a boy I once had in my class. He had the same laughing, brown eyes, but he was lost at sea during the war."

Eventually I was able to convince her that I was indeed that boy. Over tea and hot newly baked scones we had a wonderful chat about those golden years back in my childhood. As we parted, I stooped down and put my arms around that frail, old body and kissed her on the cheek. I promised her that I would keep in touch. That promise I could not keep, for sadly she died shortly after my visit. Another link with the past had gone.

Sometimes I felt that I had come back from the dead, for during the war word had gone around the island that I had been lost at sea. I found great amusement in watching the disbelief on the faces of those to whom I was introduced. My reply was always the same, "Shake hands with a ghost."

The news that I was home was soon abroad, and many of my old school friends came to see me. I found it hard to recognise those middle aged and sometimes balding men as the boys I had once known, but I too had changed in many, many ways.

The island had not changed however. It had remained untouched by the horrors of war, and by the rat race of peacetime which followed. The only change I could see was that the fathers and mothers that I had known were mostly gone. The boys with whom I had attended school now ran the crofts and farms, many of which I had worked on as a boy. I was so thankful for all this. My island was even more beautiful and peaceful than that of the image I had carried all those years. I had been afraid that, like so many of the dreams and impressions of boyhood, my dream would be shattered by the cold realities of adult life.

I wandered over the paths and fields and along the dusty roads of my childhood. As I had so often done, I sat on the heather strewn rocks and listened to the gurgling of the streams as they curled and danced over the pebbles on their way to the sea. I listened to the humming of the bees as they flitted from flower to flower and watched the vivid butterflies, adding to the rainbow of colours already surrounding me.

As the day of my departure drew nearer, I still had a boyhood ambition to fulfil. As a young and often hungry boy I used to stand outside the large hotel and watch the gentry of the day entering and leaving the premises. The aroma of food from the kitchens would drift across the still air and make my hungry stomach do somersaults. I had vowed that some day, when I was a man, I would enter that hotel, smoking the largest cigar available, sit down among the gentry and order the finest meal on the menu. In gratitude to my host, I invited him, with his wife and son, to join me for a farewell dinner in the hotel, thus fulfilling that childhood ambition. I ate more during that meal than I would have eaten in a month as a boy.

I had left a visit to my favourite rock until the day before my departure. Armed with picnic baskets, my children and I headed towards the beach. It was a glorious summer's day as we made our way up the sheep path to the summit of the rock. The scene which lay before us when we arrived at the top was breath-taking in its beauty. The sea lay below like a sheet of silver, with the sun glittering on its surface. The golden sands stretched unblemished for miles. The cattle stood up to their knees in the sea to escape the torment of the flies. My family decided to go off swimming and exploring the beach.

As I sat there, alone with my thoughts, a feeling of great contentment and peace descended on me. I gazed, once again, over those shimmering waters to the islands that lay beyond. No longer did the horizon hold any mystery for me. It was difficult indeed to believe that this beautiful, calm sea was the same angry, cruel ocean which had claimed the lives of so many thousands of brave seamen, in the dark and stormy nights of war.

My mind drifted back to the day when I had last visited this rock. I looked at the spot where my mother and I had sat. The roar of bombers, the scream of shells, the noise of huge explosions and the faces of shipmates long gone flitted across my mind. Surely my love for my wife and her love for me – all these things, war, death, fear and love – must have a meaning. God would not allow it otherwise. I now realised that God had not forsaken me in all those bitter years; I had forsaken him.

I looked again at the line where the sky met the sea. At last I had reached it; the place of understanding in the jigsaw of life, when one finds that the pieces all begin to fit and those which were missing are found. Even when the picture is complete many aspects of it will always remain a mystery.

I had been wrong to have felt so bitter over the years. Nothing in this world lasts forever; not time, not life, not even death itself, only eternity. God only lends to us. He had lent me one of his angels to give me fifteen years of happiness, and when he had taken her back he had left part of her in my children, to comfort me in my loss. I had been privileged in my life to have been given such love as I had known, and foolish to think that it could last forever.

I had never become the great sea Captain of my boyhood dreams and yet, over the years since I had lost my wife, I had become the Captain of my own ship. Like that Captain in the lifeboat, I had steered my ship through the dark and stormy seas of life, searching for a light as he had done, a light which meant the entrance to the calm safety of the harbour beyond. I could now see that light out there where the sea meets the sky. Maybe God would give me a safe course and allow me to take my ship into the safety of that harbour.

Again I thought of that last day with my mother on this very spot and of the secret she wanted to tell me. Why had I stopped her? I would never know, but in a way, I was glad that I had. I thought of the foresight and wisdom of her advice to me that day. "There is no shame in fear," she had said, but which fear had she meant? Life has so many fears: the fear of danger and death, the fear of sickness, of unemployment and poverty, to mention but a few. Many of these fears had touched my life. Had I given way to my fears? Inwardly I had often felt terrible fear. She had said that we are all born with fear and I had done my best never to show it. I had tried so hard to fulfil in my life the things she had asked of me.

My life had been little different from countless thousands of others all over the world. Some, who are born illegitimate as I was, feel shame where there is no shame. How many millions have known the pangs of hunger and poverty, of fear and pain? Very few indeed have not known the aching heart of grief, the longing for the sound of a voice that is silent forever, and the darkness of despair when all one's courage has gone and the world no longer has any meaning. Those who have walked all these dark paths have been privileged, for all these things are the ingredients of life, and without them there would be no reason and no purpose at all.

I had travelled to many far off places but I had to return to my island to find peace in my heart, and a better understanding of life. My jigsaw was complete. There were parts of the picture that I could not understand, and never would, but I had come out of the wilderness and found the Church, though the Church had done little to find me. I wondered how many more hundreds of thousands were as I had been, wandering in a wilderness of bitterness, lost and lonely and searching for a light to guide them back.

I would never know now who my father had been, but there must have been many children who had lost their fathers at sea, and they, too, must often have wondered what their fathers had been like. At least I could tell them, for I had been privileged to know them so well. In humble pride I could say of them – the Archies, the Joes, the Malkies and the Harrys – they were indeed the roughest, the toughest and the bravest men ever to go down to the sea in ships, so many thousands of them never to return. Let the generations which follow be thankful that they were such men.

For me the scars of war had healed, for I had been young, but even now I sometimes look up at a low flying plane and I think what a wonderful target it would have made. Sometimes when I see a tap dripping I find myself turning it off, and I pause and wonder why, and then I remember.

The following day, as I stood and watched my island slip into the mist astern, I thought that perhaps when my tasks are complete and my promises fulfilled, I will return to my island to spend the twilight of my life. I will listen once more to the howling of the wind and the thundering of the waves on a winter's night as they crash on the silver sands or I will sit on my rock and gaze across the sparkling sea to that line where the sky meets the sea.

Epilogue

This book tells of my father Alex's hurt and shame when at the age of twenty-three he discovered that his beloved mother Catherine was not his birth mother and that his father was unknown.

Throughout his life Alex sought to discover the identity of his birth parents, however sadly he died without ever finding out the truth that Catherine was indeed his birth mother. She had told the Tiree community he was adopted to avoid the shame of his illegitimacy.

This fact was only discovered as recently as 2015, when I researched my father's family history. A number of people who live on Tiree still remember Alex, or Michael, as he was affectionately known on the island, and they informed me that my father's great 'secret' was not a secret after all. The greatest sadness is that Alex never discovered the final piece in the jigsaw of his extraordinary life.

Alexandra Maclean